The Jeweller's Art

AN INTRODUCTION TO THE HULL GRUNDY GIFT TO THE BRITISH MUSEUM

HUGH TAIT AND CHARLOTTE GERE

PUBLISHED FOR THE TRUSTEES OF

THE BRITISH MUSEUM

BY BRITISH MUSEUM PUBLICATIONS LIMITED

ISBN 0 7141 1349 2

Published by British Museum Publications Ltd, 6 Bedford Square, London WC1B 3RA

British Library Cataloguing in Publication Data

British Museum
The jeweller's art.
1. Jewelry – Catalogs
I. Title II. Tait, Hugh III. Gere, Charlotte
739.27'09'03   NK7302.5.G72L/

Cover design
Anne Hull Grundy's Gardens: two hanging wall cases of botanical, sentimental
and Romantic jewellery, mainly dating from the period 1820–90

Designed by Sebastian Carter

Text set in 11 on 12 point Garamond and printed at
The Curwen Press, Plaistow, London

Plates printed by W. S. Cowell Ltd, Ipswich

Contents

Foreword

The British Museum's collections of jewellery, as the recent exhibition 'Jewellery through 7000 years' showed, are both rich and varied but by no means complete in their coverage of the subject. Perhaps the most conspicuous lacunae occurred in the area of European jewellery after the end of the seventeenth century. With the exception of one or two special categories, like the collections of finger-rings, cameos and engraved gems, there has been a dearth of significant acquisitions. This situation was dramatically reversed when in July 1978 Professor and Mrs Hull Grundy most generously presented their extensive collection, the greater part of which covers the period from about 1700 to 1930.

The collection is principally the product of Mrs Anne Hull Grundy's many years of experience and connoisseurship, but, in her own words, it was her husband who has always actively helped and encouraged her in her work. Mrs Hull Grundy's art-historical approach has led her to seek out documentary pieces – items bearing dates, signatures, marks, often destined to yield their full significance only after much lengthy research. Equally important, she has found items preserved in their original cases, bearing stamped or printed names of crucial significance; and so her collection of more than a thousand items, selected for their historical and artistic merits and chosen as objects 'to learn and teach from' (as Mrs Hull Grundy herself once put it), will repay continuing study and provide a basis for further research.

The Gift is to be seen, initially, in the Special Exhibitions Gallery while arrangements are being made for its permanent installation within the suite of public galleries devoted to the European decorative arts. To mark the occasion, this short Introduction to the collection has been specially prepared but a full-scale Catalogue of the Gift will be compiled in the forthcoming year. For the present, it has been necessary to be ruthlessly selective, for want of space and time, but a broad impression of the great strengths of this magnificent collection emerges from this survey.

The British Museum is, indeed, deeply indebted to Professor and Mrs Hull Grundy for their Gift, a benefaction of extraordinary generosity and of immeasurable value and pleasure both to experts and laymen alike.

TREVELYAN
Chairman of the Trustees
The British Museum

From Renaissance to Regency

Engraving was an art that developed swiftly during the fifteenth and sixteenth centuries in Europe and became a vehicle of the greatest significance for the speedy dissemination not only of Renaissance art in general but also for the enormous new repertoire of ornamental motifs based, in part at least, on classical prototypes. By about 1500 the art of engraving had already been put to use as a means for the mass reproduction of these designs, often the invention of artists of considerable stature. The prints were then sold and scattered all over Europe so that a new vocabulary of patterns and decorative motifs for almost every kind of luxury object, including jewellery, rapidly reached the workshops of goldsmiths in remote corners of Europe without the slightest need for the craftsmen to travel or look at the originals. In consequence, European jewellery, especially the fine quality court jewellery of the sixteenth and early seventeenth centuries, has an international unity of style. Only in exceptional circumstances can the identity of the country of origin of a Renaissance jewel be stated with certainty and, even more rarely, can the products of the workshop of a particular goldsmith be recognised, although many of their names are known from the account books and other documentary sources. Unfortunately, their pieces of jewellery were always unsigned and, as a result, they remain tantalisingly anonymous.

This problem is strikingly illustrated by the well-known jewelled pendant of 'Roman Charity', which was formerly in the Alfred de Rothschild, Loria and Desmoni collections before being acquired by Professor and Mrs Hull Grundy in 1960. The jewel was then published by Mrs Hull Grundy later that year alongside an engraved design by Hans Collaert of Antwerp dated 1581 and another pendant jewel of the same subject in the Rijksmuseum, Amsterdam. The engraving has long been recognised as typifying Collaert's mannerist elegance both in its figure style and in the controlled exuberance of the architectural frame and has, for example, been reproduced in Joan Evans, *History of Jewellery* (1970), and in Eric Steingraber, *Antique Jewellery* (1957). However, neither the Rijksmuseum jewel nor the Hull Grundy jewel – nor yet a third version that was on exhibition at the Baltimore Museum of Art 1962–68 from the Gutman collection – corresponds exactly. Indeed, each of the three has a different design of architectural frame and demonstrates the difficulty of attributing such jewels to any specific workshop or country, though there is general agreement that many of the jewels of this type, such as those in the Waddesdon Bequest Room of the British Museum, are probably of German origin and some were perhaps made for the Bavarian court in Munich.

In contrast, therefore, the presence of several of the finest signed engravings on silver from this period is of the greatest interest, since their authorship, date and origin is beyond dispute. The earliest (Plate 4) is an extremely rare and important work by Lambert Suavius, a leading Renaissance artist who is described in 1568 by Vasari, in his 'Life of Marcantorio', as 'an excellent engraver on copper'. He was born in Liège about 1510 with the surname Suterman, which he appears to have preferred in a latinised form; active in Liège and Antwerp in the two decades from 1540 to 1560, he died in 1567. Whereas he is well-known for his fine prints, few other silver plaques by Suavius seem to have been recorded. Furthermore, this roundel is conceived as a work of art in its own right since any print taken from it would reproduce the inscription in reverse. This silver disc was apparently made to commemorate the Peace of Cateau-Cambrésis, which was concluded on 5 April

1559, and was an event of major political importance, for with it the French struggle for the possession of Italy (Milan, Sicily and Naples) ceased – at least, until the Napoleonic Wars nearly two and a half centuries later. The war between France and Spain had broken out in 1556 but in the following year the French were overwhelmingly defeated by forces from the Spanish Netherlands on the northern borders; however, the French gained one victory during the war for in 1558 the English were finally driven out of Calais and were never again to possess territory on the mainland of France. The engraving, which with its pair of doves and its laurels and its inscription is concerned with the theme of peace between Spain and its adversary, France, is a masterly essay in the Renaissance style, drawing heavily on classical sources, though the treatment of the figures reveals the influence of the Italian Mannerist school, particularly of the Italian painters working for the French court at Fontainebleau.

Lambert Suavius's works include several engraved portraits of eminent contemporaries but among the small collection of his works in the Prints and Drawings Department of the British Museum there is one print of a portrait in reverse; acquired in 1867, this print was presumably taken from a silver medallion, designed as a work of art – not as a means for mass reproduction. Three such portrait medallions of silver signed by Simon de Passe are rare works of art (Plate 2). This artist, son of Crispin de Passe, the Elder, came to England from the Low Countries in about 1615–16 but within ten years he had moved to the Danish court in Copenhagen, where he died in 1647, aged fifty-two. Little has come to light about his sojourn in London but like his Dutch compatriot, Arnold Lulls, who designed jewellery for James I and his Queen, Anne of Denmark, Simon de Passe probably enjoyed royal patronage. Certainly, his prints include portraits of English monarchs, including James I and his Consort, as well as most of the luminaries of the Jacobean court including Robert Carr and Buckingham. Unlike his copper-plates which would have been engraved in reverse, these three silver pendant medallions of Elizabeth I, James I and Maria of Austria, are not intended for printing and on the back of the portrait of Maria, the artist has not only added to his signature the word '*Lond.*' (for London), but has engraved the identical inscription twice, once in French and once in English. Interest in Maria of Austria, the Spanish Infanta, was at its height at King James's court in London during the negotiations for a marriage between Prince Charles and Philip III's daughter, which were formally opened in the spring of 1617 and abandoned by late 1623. Several examples of each of these portrait medallions have been recorded and there is considerable debate about the technique that Simon de Passe may have employed in order to obtain such similar results. A close study and detailed comparison of the Queen Elizabeth I and the James I medallions with a second examplar has established that, although almost every minute line is repeated, there are a few very minor differences, which may be sufficient to convince future scholars that Simon de Passe did not reproduce these silver portrait medallions by some mechanical method. The degree of accuracy with which each repeats the engraving of the other exemplar is, however, a veritable *tour de force* if it were executed in an entirely free-hand manner, relying solely on the eye.

The application of the art of engraving for purely decorative purposes to silver jewellery of this period can be seen on a number of lockets and other items of jewellery. Perhaps the finest of its type is the devotional pendant locket (Plate 4), which opens to reveal two painted miniatures, which, like the elaborately engraved scenes on the exterior, are in a markedly German or Netherlandish style. The lively border, engraved with a certain verve, seems more French in origin and no doubt is yet another example of how quickly this kind of ornament spread to other countries. This same phenomenon can be seen on an almost contemporary Netherlandish silver book-cover in the Hull Grundy Gift, for the engraved openwork pattern, inhabited by birds, is ultimately of French origin. Fortunately, a similar book-cover in the Rijksmuseum, Amsterdam, contains a delicately engraved scene of St Jerome in the Desert, which can be firmly attributed to the Netherlandish school at the beginning of the seventeenth century.

At about the same time, probably in England, a goldsmith created shallow troughs in each of the oblong octagonal links of this gold chain (Plate 5). The dark substance laid into these channels has been described as pitch but as no particle has yet been analysed it must remain a question of great interest. No other example has been recorded, though the inlaying of wood in gold religious jewellery (rosaries, etc.) is known in the seventeenth and eighteenth centuries – an example is preserved in the Hull Grundy collection – and the effect from a distance is not dissimilar.

Even more difficult to date and locate are Professor Hull Grundy's very interesting group of three silver and one gold spherical containers (Plate 5), which range in length from 4·6 cm. to 10·2 cm., the largest being the gold container. They are all of the same ovoid spherical form, opening in two halves but having no hinge, catch or fastening device; the simple design relies on the moulded band on one half fitting over the lip of the companion half sufficiently tightly to keep it closed. The interior surfaces, though smooth, show the hammer marks quite plainly but the exterior surfaces in each case are covered by an openwork scrolling foliate ornament, executed in applied thin strips of silver. The surface of this ornament is engraved but the elementary hatching gives only a summary definition to the leaves, etc. The inconclusive Anglo-Indian provenance of one of two similar containers in the Department of Oriental Antiquities throws no light on their place of origin. The impression of filigree-work is deceptive, and may account for the earlier attribution of the objects to Turkish workshops of the eighteenth century. Similar work can be seen, however, in English and Continental watches of the seventeenth century, especially in the applied ornament on the back-plates of the movements.

Such a date would be in keeping with the uses to which these objects are believed to have been put. It is thought that they were made to hold bezoar stones – calcareous concretions impregnated with gallic acid formed in the stomach of various animals: the Persian wild goat, ibex, certain kinds of deer, monkeys, the llama of Peru and its congeners. The concretions vary in size from a small bird's egg to a coconut. The name is of Persian derivation, transmitted to the West through the Arabs, and means literally 'without poison'. It was believed that the creatures in whose stomachs these concretions formed had been bitten by serpents or scorpions, and that they had then eaten a sovereign herb: 'which having eaten they are presently cured, but the substance of the herb converteth itself into a medicinal stone' (Hawkins's account of the voyage of 1593). The range of efficacy was extended from specific cases of poisoning to every kind of disorder from indigestion to epilepsy, all being set down to the action of some venomous influence. Burton in his *Anatomy* even recommends it because 'it hath an especial virtue against all melancholy affections'. A few grains of the bezoar were taken in water, either alone or with other substances. The high medicinal value ascribed to these objects naturally enhanced their value and Sir Thomas Roe, writing in 1614, gives the price in England as three pounds an ounce, or more. Clearly, only the rich could afford whole bezoar stones and it is not surprising, therefore, to find them mounted in gold and silver, even worn as a pendant around the neck, like the one preserved in the Kunsthistorisches Museum, Vienna, which is encased in delicate gold filigree of early seventeenth century date. Indeed, they appear in the inventories of the Renaissance princes and frequently are listed among the jewels. James 1 of England possessed 'one great Bezar stone sett in gould, which was Queen Elizabeth's'.

No doubt it was an extension of this custom that led Englishmen, like Dr John King at St John's College, Oxford, and Samuel Pepys in London, to preserve in gold and silver cases the stones that had been successfully removed from their own bodies. Medical operations were extremely hazardous in the seventeenth century and to have survived was worth commemorating in this way, but whether these spherical containers were ever used for this latter purpose is uncertain.

After the Renaissance, the services of the engraver continued to be employed for the enrichment of the appearance of jewellery but often, as the examples in the Hull Grundy Gift demonstrate, in a relatively minor capacity. An outstandingly good illustration from the middle of the eighteenth century is the splendid Badge of the Anti-Gallican Society where the task of the engraver was merely to repeat on the silver-gilt panels of the back of the Badge (Plate 3), the heraldic device of the Society and the representation of Britannia that so colourfully decorate the front (Plate III). Nevertheless, the unobstrusive use of the rococo scroll-work gives a highly decorative finish to the back of this jewel, which was probably intended to be worn by one of the Grand Presidents of the Society, such as Sir Stephen Theodore Janssen, the principal proprietor of the Battersea Enamel Works at York House, Battersea, and in 1754–55 Lord Mayor of London. The Society was formed in London when Anglo-French rivalry both in the political and the commercial fields was reaching a peak and its avowed intention was to oppose and prevent the importation of French goods and manufactures.

The Society's badge reflects its objectives for it depicts St George on horseback piercing with his spear a shield bearing the three *fleurs-de-lys* of France. The Supporters are the lion rampant of England on the left and the double-headed eagle of Austria on the right, for the British were the allies of Maria Theresa in the War of the Austrian Succession and George II, the last British monarch to command his army in the field, defeated the French at Dettingen in 1743. The Peace of Aix-la-Chapelle in 1748 solved few problems, least of all the bitter commercial rivalry and so the Society continued to flourish long after the War had ended.

The use of the technique of enamelling to add richness and colour to jewellery had reached a pinnacle of excellence during the Renaissance, especially in the hands of Benvenuto Cellini (1500–71), perhaps the greatest goldsmith of that era. In his technical *Treatise*, Cellini describes with what slow and painstaking skill he modelled and enamelled miniature sculptural scenes in relief to vie with the creations of his great rival, Caradosso (died 1527). He devotes a lengthy section to describing the enamelling techniques he favoured but, tragically, no jewellery by Cellini appears to have survived. Among the anonymous creations in the Hull Grundy Gift there is a Spanish pendant cross of the early seventeenth century (Plate 1), decorated with both opaque and translucent enamels of various colours. On the back, executed in relief and enamelled, is the applied gold figure of the Virgin Mary standing on a crescent moon, the iconographical representation of the Virgin of the Immaculate Conception. During the second decade of the century, the public fervour and clamour in Spain, particularly in Seville, for the proclamation of the conception of the Virgin as immaculate became intense and despite the Inquisition issuing a decree in 1647 banning the term, its use continued. However, there is evidence in royal inventories of the late sixteenth century that gold pendants of the Virgin of the Immaculate Conception had already been made for the Spanish court.

A new form of enamelling can be seen on the back of a most spectacular Spanish gold pendant set with table-cut emeralds (Plate I). An opaque white enamel has been fired on to the entire surface of the reverse of this jewel and on to the white ground has been painted, in several coloured enamels, a simple naturalistic form of decoration. The first exponents of this technique appear to have been two Frenchmen, Jean and Henri Toutin, in the second quarter of the seventeenth century and it is especially important to discover a jewel of undoubted Spanish origin dating from the middle of the century on which this technique has been employed. The jewel is made in two parts, the lower half incorporates in the flowing openwork design, the initial 'S' impaled with a nail – a symbol used in Spain to denote membership of a religious confraternity. The goldsmith's fluid design triumphs over the eye-catching quality of the emeralds by virtue of its masterly use of harmonious naturalistic and curvilinear elements. The fashion in Spain was for one enormous jewel of great splendour, occasionally accompanied by earrings to match; in this instance, the original owner commissioned a masterpiece.

The early Toutin technique of painting on a white enamel ground, thereby producing miniatures in enamel, became very popular at the French court and soon was copied in Holland. A mid-seventeenth century necklace composed of small plaques (Plate 7), each painted in a warm sepia monochrome with minute landscape scenes incorporating buildings and tiny figures, seems to be of Dutch origin. Indeed, the landscapes are reminiscent of the Italianising Dutch 'Bambocchiante' painters working in the style of Claude Lorraine. On the reverse the necklace has a gaily coloured floral decoration, mainly done in yellows and light green, which is so characteristic of Dutch and South German enamelled trinkets and *objets de vertu* in the third quarter of the seventeenth century.

With far greater *finesse* and in true miniaturist style, the unknown painter of the 'Judith in the Tent of Holophernes' enamel (Plate 6) has created a tiny *chef d'oeuvre*. Using only one colour, a reddish sepia, the enameller has achieved subtle effects of modelling and of light and shade by using the stipple technique in conjunction with the more traditional method. Stippling involves building up various densities of colour or highlights of brightness by increasing or diminishing the number of minute dots. Another very accomplished example, using a wide range of colours, is 'The Rape of Helen' (Plate 6), which adorns the back of an enamelled watch-case that was subsequently most skilfully and attractively converted into a box. Whilst it is difficult to be certain how the art of painting on enamel was introduced into Geneva, there is no doubt that among the first to practise this craft were the French Huguenot refugees. The Huaud family is an excellent example: Pierre I (*c.* 1620–80) was a goldsmith and enameller of Chatellerault, who came to Geneva in 1630. Pierre II (1647–1700), known as Huaud l'Aîné, and the two Huaud brothers (Jean-Pierre 1655–1723 and Ami 1657–1724) continued to dominate the Swiss production of enamelled watch-cases into the eighteenth century but few of these later pieces can match the excellence of this 'Rape of Helen' case in the Hull Grundy Gift.

In England the art of miniature painting in enamels was introduced to the court of Charles I by the gifted Jean Petitot, of Geneva, but he returned to the Continent before the Civil War began. It took another foreign artist, Charles Boit (1663–1727), a Swedish jeweller whose father was French, to revitalise the art in England. He arrived in London in 1687 and during the reigns of William and Mary and Queen Anne produced many excellent miniature portraits in enamel. None is more impressive than that of Sidney Godolphin (Plate II), who was created Earl of Godolphin in 1706. This signed work is after the Kneller portrait at Blenheim, which shows the sitter in his Garter robes. The artist, Charles Boit, is often regarded as the founder of the British school of enamel painters and this portrait in the Hull Grundy collection exemplifies his great qualities. It also introduces one to another rare and fine technique – the art of *piqué*. The Boit portrait is set inside the lid of an oval tortoiseshell box most beautifully decorated with gold *piqué-point*.

Two very similar oval tortoiseshell boxes decorated with fine gold *piqué-point* (Plate IV, below) adequately convey the beauties of this minor art. The term *piqué* is generally used to embrace all kinds of gold and silver inlaid decoration on luxury objects, usually made of tortoiseshell. In England the fine 'hair-line' *piqué* often appears on watch-cases of the middle and late seventeenth century; there is an example of this form – an early tortoiseshell teapoy – in the Hull Grundy collection. In France, Charles Boulle (1642–1732) is often credited with turning the craft into an art but, as with the enamellers, some *piqué* workers fled abroad at the time of the Revocation of the Edict of Nantes in 1685 and took their skills to other countries; as a result, it is not always possible to identify the country of origin. The most exquisite form of *piqué* is executed entirely in '*petites et gros points*' and is usually dated to the late period of Louis XIV's reign. The two examples, like the box with the Boit portrait of Sidney Godolphin, probably date from around 1700 and are particularly fine illustrations of the use of tiny gold nails of graduated sizes to build up a subtle effect, which is at its most successful in the oriental or *chinoiserie* design on the lid of the Godolphin box.

The wonderful effect of fine gold *piqué-point* on ivory can be seen on the base of the most unusual and beautiful, carved, shallow box (Plate IV, above). The sides and the lid are decorated not only in gold *piqué-point* but with applied gold animals, trees and, most noticeably, the rays of the sun; all the applied elements are carefully placed within a landscape, carved in low relief. This exceptional combination may be unique and, with all its allusions to the court of the 'Sun King' hidden in its innocent decoration, could have been made in Paris when the art was at its height in the 1680s.

Less exceptional but nevertheless highly prized is the combination of *blonde* tortoiseshell and gold *piqué-point*, which seems to have been at the height of fashion at the end of Louis xiv's reign and during the *Régence*. The example in the Hull Grundy collection (Plate II) is embellished with an enamelled gold thumb-piece of elegant design and supreme craftmanship.

Towards the end of Louis xiv's reign there was an increasing vogue for *piqué-posé* ('strip' decoration in gold or silver), and a fine box with this engraved silver work combined with silver *piqué-point* decoration is included in the Gift (Plate IV below). Another box (Plate IV, above) has the gold *piqué-point* enhanced by the use of engraved mother-of-pearl and inlaid chased gold 'strips' (*piqué-posé*). The effect is more pictorial and less elegant but its widespread popularity endured into the second half of the eighteenth century, even among the box-makers of Paris.

Mother-of-pearl was a material ideally suited to the tastes of the eighteenth century. In a *Régence* double miniature case (Plate IV), mother-of-pearl has been used to act as a bright foil to the chased and pierced gold work and in the bands of open trellis-work of mother-of-pearl, the background is gold, thereby creating a reverse effect. This subtle miniature work on gold, using fine chasing tools to create tiny figures and minute scenes, was developed during the *Régence* and was soon copied in England.

The gold and mother-of-pearl box (Plate II) is unmarked but is probably English and dates from George ii's reign. Its fine *ciselé* ornament lacks the extreme delicacy of the Paris masters but is executed with skill and understanding of form. Two more handsome English gold boxes (Plate IV) illustrate the development away from the flat surface *ciselé* work towards high relief; at the same time, the earlier emphasis on borders and formal strapwork frames disappears until the scene in relief fills the surface from edge to edge.

At the French court, boxes of three or, even, four different colours of gold became increasingly fashionable after the middle decades of the century and it is wonderful to have in the Gift a unique object in three-coloured gold. It is a tambour-hook holder (Plate 10), such as Madame de Pompadour may be seen holding in the well-known portrait by Drouais. Her enjoyment of this pastime no doubt caused many to follow suit and the quality of the engine-turned decoration is worthy of the French court.

In contrast, the ivory *nécessaire* (Plate 10) with its gold *piqué-point* is less grand but equally functional. In its simple form and restrained decoration, this object of practical use has become an object that also pleases the eye. Fortunately, it has survived with most of its original instruments and so complements the exciting discovery of the courtly tambour-hook holder. The latter is, also, both beautifully proportioned and yet designed to unscrew into three sections, with a reversible section that screws into the head of the holder. Gold tambour-hook holders of the eighteenth century seem not to have survived unless, like this one, they are waiting to be recognised.

Equally well-executed is the cylindrical pendant cross (Plate II) composed of polished hard-stones of varied colours set in gold. Technically perfect, this cross is also remarkable for its design and, in the absence of marks or signatures, the attribution of this cross to a workshop in Dresden, where both Taddel and Neuber excelled in this art of the lapidary/goldsmith, does seem reasonable. Other centres, especially Geneva in Switzerland, were also polishing a fascinating variety of hard-stones for their goldsmiths to mount but the excellence of this cross seems to be superior to the products of these other centres and to have the attributes of a Dresden court object.

Even more unexpected is the beautiful purple glass pendant (Plate 6), for it would seem that the painted decoration lies, not on the surface, but within the glass. Apparently, after the miniature scene was painted onto the oval purple glass, it was overlaid with a layer of clear glass, which appears to take on the purple colour beneath and yet does not distort the colours of the miniature painting because it is a clear glass. Curiously, the two birds were not painted by the miniaturist but added, using gold itself to catch the eye. The style and palette make an early eighteenth century date in France most probable, though few examples of comparable French decorative glass of the end of Louis xiv's reign have survived.

Yet a further *tour-de-force* in light-hearted mood is the English ivory box (Plate 11) with its charming ivory carving in the lid seen against a pink foil background. The carving is so thin that the pink background colour is reflected back through the ivory. The Cupid, who is pulling the ship into harbour, has a witty text under his feet but no hidden signature. It was generally believed that this kind of delicate work was the special achievement of John Voyez, who in 1775 left Staffordshire 'to go and make paste seals in London', but there is a dearth of reliable evidence. The minute ivories bearing the signatures of Stephany and Dresch are among the closest related material. Established in London, they exhibited at the Royal Academy in the late eighteenth century, and may have been responsible for some similar items in the Gift.

No such problem exists with the magnificent gift of the Prince Regent to his famous chef, John Watier (Plate 11). This handsome box of tortoiseshell has a gold lid enclosing under glass a gold medallic head of the Prince silhouetted against a vibrant blue translucent enamel laid over engine-turned gold; on either side, the finely chased gold setting incorporates the Prince of Wales's Feathers and Coronet and typifies the taste of Regency London in 1815. It was in this year, according to the inscription engraved on the gold surface of the underside of the lid, that this box was given to John Watier. He founded one of London's renowned gaming clubs in 1807; it lasted until 1819, famed as much for its excellent food as for its extravagant gambling.

Of particular importance for the students of medallic art is the very fine head of the Prince in gold, for it is signed by the modeller, Rouw, as well as the engraver, Barber. The latter's signature appears on the well-known medal commemorating the Peace in 1814, but the identity of the modeller has hitherto been untraced. Because of the close similarities between the two heads, despite the addition of a laurel wreath on the 1814 medal, there is now no doubt that Rouw was responsible for this exceptional portrait of the Prince in 1814. No other example of the version on the Watier box is recorded and, no doubt, the Prince himself was responsible for its very limited use.

While the gentlemen of the eighteenth century besported themselves with snuff-boxes and gem-set Badges of Orders and Societies (Plate III), the ladies were resplendent, bedecked in that other facet of the jeweller's art, the gem-encrusted sprays, aigrettes and brooches (Plate V). In jewellery of this kind the beauty of the gem-stones and the skill of the gem-cutter tends to take precedence but the designer and the jeweller whose skilful settings maximises the merits of the stones have no less important roles to play than in the days of Cellini.

Romanticism to Art-Nouveau

At the end of the eighteenth century the character of the Hull Grundy Gift alters significantly. Here the range, both technically and historically is very much greater, reflecting changing fashions in a way that is impossible in the earlier period where surviving pieces tend to be of greater historical significance and of less relevance to the story of taste. It is inevitable that the lesser pieces from any period should be the first to disappear. Whereas our knowledge of Royal jewels from the sixteenth and seventeenth centuries is reasonably comprehensive, it is only through the fortuitous survival in strange circumstances of the Cheapside Hoard in the City of London that we have any clear idea of the form and technique of those lesser pieces which were presumably the everyday ornaments of the prosperous merchant class. Greater respect for the minutiae of historical evidence has ensured the present day concern with the preservation of fashionable trinkets and ornaments with no intrinsic value, but not before much had already been lost, consigned to the dustbin or the melting pot.

Some hint of the extent to which fashion in dress and jewellery design had already begun to interact is vouchsafed in the group of gem-set and paste ornaments dating from the late seventeenth and the eighteenth centuries (Plate V). So much gem-set jewellery has inevitably been altered to conform with changing taste that it is unusual to find pieces set with diamonds, rubies, emeralds or any rare precious stones which even approximate to their original form, as do the aigrettes and hair-ornaments in this collection (Plates 8, 9). With the late eighteenth century aigrette in gold and diamonds (Plate 9), the detachable pin has survived as well, enabling us to understand the mechanics for wearing these ornaments, which is of course not apparent from contemporary portraits where they are shown in use. With such a wide spectrum of materials and techniques it is possible to construct a rough picture of the distribution through the various social classes of these ornaments, ranging from the diamond-set pieces through the garnet jewels to the pastes and 'Vauxhall' glass, iron pyrites and cut-steel, though it is apparent that paste jewellery was owned and worn by members of the Court circle in the eighteenth century. Mrs Delany's *Letters* are full of speculations as to the value of many of the pieces she saw worn at Court functions which she attended. The existence of a large range of comparative material in such a variety of techniques allows one to arrive at some idea of dating, which with undocumented pieces is usually necessarily very vague. Much can be learned from observing the growing sophistication of technique in lapidary work and in gem-setting in this particular group of pieces, which demonstrates the development of the modern technique in diamond setting with its emphasis on the refraction of light, achieved partly through the evolution of the highly refractive brilliant-cut and partly through the adoption of the *à jour* or open-backed setting.

The emphasis on fashion in jewellery design coincides with the increasing importance of gem-setting and the decline in the use of enamelled ornamentation of the settings which dates from the beginning of the eighteenth century. This preoccupation with gems widened the gap between fine art and applied art, a situation which was to be even more strongly emphasised during the next hundred years with the development of the jewelled dress ornament. The fashionable, diamond-set knots and bows, bouquets and feathers are ludicrously grand substitutes for ribbon and feathers and real flowers; their whole conception is essentially frivolous and is thus far removed in spirit from the gold and enamelled sculptural pendants of the Renaissance. The tradition of making jewelled dress accessories carried on well into the nineteenth century. The bouquet and flower spray comb-mounts and brooches are again precious re-creations of the fashionable fresh or artificial flower-bouquets which were widely worn in the evening during the period 1800–40 (Plates 16, 17).

Of great historical interest and far from frivolous in conception is the cameo or engraved gem, which can be seen as a miniature work of sculpture, conveniently portable and sometimes set as a personal ornament; these are known to have been treasured by their owners, often in preference to the more intrinsically valuable gem-set pieces. This remarkable group of cameos (Plates X, XI) has a different relevance for the British Museum than the rest of the collection. The Museum holds the national collection of cameos, a comprehensive survey of the art of gem-engraving from the earliest period, which, owing to its archaeological bias, is least strong in the post-Renaissance. In the eighteenth and nineteenth centuries the collection is very much less than representative, and the cameos and intaglios in the Hull Grundy Gift complement the Museum's holdings in a most valuable way. Some of the gem-engravers in this group, which includes a very high proportion of signed pieces, were not previously represented in the collection. For instance, neither Tommaso Saulini nor his son were included; both are represented by signed works of high quality in the Hull Grundy Gift (Plate X). The same is true of Charles Bacon, working in the first half of the nineteenth century, here represented by a fine intaglio of a classical male head. N. Mastini is another useful addition, being an engraver identified by Ernst Kris as a separate personality from Angelo and Nicolo Amastini, with whom he was previously confused. The only signed gem in the British Museum collection by Philippo Rega was destroyed by enemy action while on exhibition in 1941, therefore the two examples of his work in the Hull Grundy Gift repair a sad loss (Plate XI). Rega became the head of the Naples mint and presumably cut the fine portrait head of Admiral Lord Nelson in about 1798 at the time of the Italian Campaign against Napoleon. The ring with a bezel in the form of a neo-classical reversed glass intaglio signed by Charles Brown is a rare, possibly even unique, example of his work in this technique. There is no example in the Hermitage (where there is a large collection of works by William and Charles Brown) nor in the British Museum. Although signed works by Morelli and Girometti exist in the Museum's collection their number was also depleted by the destruction of the exhibition gallery in 1941, and the present examples are again valuable additions (Plate XI). The Royal portrait cameos of George III (Plate XI) and George IV, and the fine intaglio ring-stone, also of George IV, by Benedetto Pistrucci not only provide very fine examples of his mastery of the portrait cameo, but relate to coins of the realm, notably the 1816 guinea, which was cut from the portrait cameo by Thomas Wyon, the younger, thus providing a link between two important Museum collections, the cameos and coins and medals. The high proportion of signed pieces is of great value in making comparative attributions in an area where difficult problems of naming and dating still exist.

The group of 'Berlin' ironwork is also of considerable historical and technical interest (Plate 15). It is always said to have been originally conceived to compensate those German patriots who gave up their gold to finance the defence of their country during the Napoleonic wars, and then to have become fashionable as a jewellery material in its own right. 'Berlin' ironwork seems from recent research to have an earlier history than this traditional belief suggests; there is evidence of its manufacture in Silesia in the eighteenth century and a suggestion has been made that it was also made in France from the late 1780s. There are a number of examples inscribed 'Gold gab ich fur Eisen 1813' (I gave gold for iron), which confirm that ironwork ornaments were used for this purpose, but it seems likely that the trade already existed – indeed it would be very remarkable if such a complex and refined technique could have been quickly developed to meet an emergency of war in this way, having been intended for mourning jewellery. It was certainly worn as such in the nineteenth century, but its primary interest must have been as a technological curiosity. The existence of a Berlin ironwork fan – a palpably absurd use of the material since it would certainly have fractured if put to use very frequently – tends to confirm this. The fan was made for the Great Exhibition in London in 1851, and it is interesting to note that a surprising number of exhibits, notably amongst the jewellery, survive from this occasion. It must be assumed that a category of object exists, made specially for the purposes of exhibiting at these great trade shows, which has no real relevance to this history of personal taste, and which was never put to use.

The difficulties of reconciling the two possibilities inherent in jewellery design, the piece seen essentially as a miniature work of art, or primarily as a personal ornament are nowhere more apparent than in the historical revival styles which became popular in the mid-nineteenth century. The inspiration for these pieces comes mainly from works of art, either in the form of early jewels adapted from surviving originals, from portraits, or from sculptural and ornamental motifs in architecture. These sources are not the stuff of which wearable personal ornaments can be made, many of these nineteenth century pastiches of ancient jewellery must have had a primarily documentary interest to the owners. Here again we are faced with the inevitable logic of archaeological survival, that the things which remain undamaged and unaltered are those least likely to have been in everyday use, and thus least likely to present us with a useful undistorted picture of the period in which they were made. The Victorians have a reputation for preferring unwearably heavy jewellery, which is clearly the inevitable result of the survival of a great many heavy unwearable pieces, and we are once again presented with a detailed and easily documented view of only part of the picture. The group of historical revival jewellery in this collection is unusually comprehensive, presenting an unrivalled picture of the stylistic and technical experiments of the nineteenth century craftsmen, and including work by hitherto unknown or very unfamiliar names. While most people who are interested in the jewellery of the nineteenth century will certainly have heard of Castellani – and the group of pieces by him is of unusual range and technical quality (Plates VI, XII) – they may well not be so familiar with the work of Giacinto Melillo or Ernesto Pierret (Plates 21–23), both goldsmiths working in the same manner as Castellani and with equal technical brilliance who are represented in this collection by marked pieces. The work of Carli and Fiorentino, both again represented by marked examples (Plate IX), is again close to that of the Castellani family, emphasising the point that attribution to a particular workshop unsupported by incontestable evidence is very dangerous. Eugène Fontenay and Jules Wièse will probably again be less familiar names than F. D. Froment-Meurice, all here represented by characteristic works (Plate XIII), as are a group of English and Irish archaeological and historical designers, whose sources provide an illuminating insight into the passionate interest manifested in the mid-nineteenth century in archaeological discoveries. The rare 'Assyrian' brooch (Plate 23) has a central plaque ornamented with an almost exact copy of an Assyrian relief from the throne room of Ashurnasipal, discovered in the course of his excavations at Nimrud by Sir Austen Layard, and published by him in 1849. The circular shawl-pins by the Irish jewellers, Waterhouse and West of Dublin, are based on Celtic ring brooches which were excavated in the nineteenth century (Plate 25). The so-called 'Tara' brooch was found in 1850 and came into the possession of Messrs Waterhouse, who were ready with copies in time for the Great Exhibition in London in the following year.

The relationship between archaeological discoveries and jewellery design can provide useful evidence for dating pieces. This is of particular value in the case of the Castellani firm where dating is very difficult; while there is some help to be gained from studying a sequence in the use of marks it does not allow for great precision in the activities of a firm whose involvement in the field of archaeological revival jewellery spans nearly a hundred years. Two of the pieces in this collection have stylistic connections with jewels which must have been well known to the Castellanis, one of which was, indeed, in their own collection. The design of the gold sun-burst or 'Helios' brooch

(Plate 21) is taken from a Greek third century brooch or earring in the Campana collection, which is now in the Louvre. This great collection, formed by the Cavaliere Campana and sold to the French Government in 1861, was certainly known to the Castellanis who, according to Henri Vever (*La Bijouterie Française du XIXᵉ siècle*, 1902–8) were acting as agents in the sale. He specifies an otherwise obscure brother, Giulielgmo, as the principal agent between the two parties. It seems reasonable to suggest that the Castellani 'Helios' brooch was made, or at least the design was conceived, before the Hellenistic original left Italy, and although the date of 1860 cannot be put forward as unquestionably correct it probably indicates the area fairly accurately. The other piece in this collection which is connected in design with a surviving ancient jewel is the 'Agnus Dei' brooch (Plate VI). Although the mosiac-work centre is taken from a well-known prototype in Ravenna, the enamelled border ornamentation is based on the similar enamel work bordering the rare Early Christian brooch known as the 'Castellani' brooch which was bought from the Castellani family by the British Museum in 1865. Again it seems logical to assume that the design of the 'Agnus Dei' brooch was conceived in the early 'sixties before the British Museum's 'Castellani' brooch left the family. Other evidence for dating pieces can be put together from the most disparate sources; with the neo-Gothic pectoral cross (Plate XII) the attribution to Burges is supported by a contemporary illustration of this very piece. However, the probable dating of the marked Carlo Doria Tudor style cross (Plate 24), is arrived at in a more complex way through tracing the origins of the design, which is based, with some alterations, on a cruciform pendant worn by the sitter (said to be the young Elizabeth 1) in an anonymous portrait in the Royal Collection which was lent by Queen Victoria to the Portrait Exhibition at South Kensington in 1866. At that time the portrait was attributed to Holbein, which made it an ideal source for a 'Holbeinesque' jewel. A number of versions of this cross were made, as is shown by the related, but greatly altered, piece (Plate 24) marked R.P., for Robert Phillips. There seems to be no doubt of the connection between the mysterious Carlo Doria, who remains a completely elusive figure, and the Phillips firm in Cockspur Street. It is interesting to have these two related pieces, the one bearing Doria's mark, and the other the Robert Phillips mark which was entered at Goldsmiths' Hall in 1851 for use on the firm's silverware and is only very rarely found on the jewellery. Doria's mark also appears on the gold setting of the large 'Roma' cameo cut in the Saulini studio (Plate X). Here again, from external evidence, the dating can be rather precise. Tommaso Saulini showed a stone version of the 'Roma' cameo at the 1862 International Exhibition in London; shell versions, of which this cameo is an example, were available for sale to the public, and it seems likely that the purchaser of this cameo simply took it to Phillips's shop in Cockspur Street and ordered a setting for it at the time when he bought it.

In spite of the abundance of evidence in the form of stylistic influence, use of a rare and difficult technique and a well-known and well-documented maker's mark, the Japanese style locket-case (Plate XV), bearing the mark of Alexis Falize is very hard to date precisely. Henri Vever (*op. cit.*) gives a long account of the firm taken from Alexis Falize's son Lucien. The evidence he presents seems to suggest that the spectacular cloisonné pieces, of which a small number of variable quality still survive, were made by Lucien, and one would have no reason to doubt this were it not for the fact that Vever himself seems to feel somewhat uneasy with the story as it was told to him. The captions to the illustrations of the Falize cloisonné-work are rather evasive, some crediting Lucien and giving dates, others not. Another side of the story is provided by the contemporary documentation which is attached to some ambitious pieces of the Maison Falize's cloisonné-work jewellery in public collections in this country: a necklace in the Victoria and Albert Museum, London, acquired in 1869 was ascribed to the father, Alexis; a set of necklace and earrings in the Ashmolean Museum, Oxford, was bought in Paris in 1867 from Alexis Falize. The mark of the firm, 'AF' with a flail, was used even after the retirement of Alexis and it is possible that this piece could belong to the group exhibited by Lucien in 1876 (the year in which he took over the firm), but it seems to belong stylistically to the earlier group, and has therefore been, tentatively, given an earlier date and ascribed to the hand of Alexis Falize.

While the artist responsible for this cloisonné piece may still be a matter for dispute, there can be no doubt about the source of inspiration. A mania for Japanese art, starting in 1858, when the opening up of the long-closed trade route to Japan by the American, Commander Perry, provided material for the decoration of objects of every kind, jewellery being no exception. Tiffany & Co. of New York were fortunate in having, in Edward Moore, a director who was a knowledgeable collector of Japanese art objects, and it is due to him that their excursions into the field of 'Japonisme' are so successful (Plate XV). He was also instrumental in ensuring the very high standard of technique in the metalworking – a special talent of the Japanese, notably the sword-makers – by employing Japanese craftsmen in the Tiffany workshops. The examples of this type of work by Tiffany in the Gift are very fine, showing a mastery of the use of three- and four-colour gold which is rare in most of the Japanese-inspired jewellery to emerge from commercial workshops at this period, and it must be assumed that the use of Japanese craftsmen is crucial in this respect.

In the context of dating jewellery from marks and inscriptions it seems appropriate to mention that inscriptions can be misleading. They are frequently added later, and where they do not seem to fit with the style of the piece in question they should be disregarded as evidence of exact dating.

There seems to be no question that historical revival jewellery of this kind was widely admired, but there is little evidence (either from portraits or contemporary commentary) that these pieces were much worn. Henri Vever, in his invaluable work, *La Bijouterie Française du XIXe Siècle*, illustrates three photographs, of the Empress Eugènie, of Princess Alice and of the Comtesse de Castiglione in jewels of archaeological inspiration, but these are rare exceptions. An equally rare instance of a pendant in the neo-Renaissance style being worn occurs in a portrait of the Empress Frederick of Germany (Queen Victoria's eldest daughter, the Princess Royal), by Heinrich von Angeli (now in the Wallace Collection), but it is not exactly identifiable with any particular piece as the detail is insufficiently precise. A contributor to *Punch*, the humorous periodical, thought that the idea of anyone actually wearing Castellani's archaeological revival jewellery was so hilarious that he devoted a considerable amount of space to ironic comment, explaining the caricature of a young girl ludicrously over-burdened with earrings in the form of winged goddesses, bullas, chains and pins, which appeared in June 1859.

Another group of pieces which have been conceived almost as miniature sculptures, are the chased gold dragon and chimera brooches, popular in France in the 'seventies and 'eighties (Plate 27). Three firms are known to have made pieces in this manner: Jules Wièse, Maison Robin and Maison Plissen & Hartz, but it has also been suggested that they were designed by some of the *animalier* sculptors of the period, notably associates of Barye and Mêne. There is some evidence to suggest that similar chased gold pieces were made in England – one of the eagle brooches in this collection is signed 'A. Simey' – and in the Austro-Hungarian Empire. The use of sculptors to design jewels has many precedents in France in the nineteenth century, and was to become almost commonplace at the turn of the century.

The development at the end of the nineteenth century of the Art-Nouveau style (Plate 32) was to usher in yet another period of experiment with the idea of the jewel conceived as a miniature work of art. The use of certain techniques gives a clue to the designer's attitude, particularly in the pieces using *plique-à-jour* open-backed enamel, where the effect of the light shining through the coloured enamels is lost when the piece is worn. It is very unlikely that Lalique ever envisaged anyone wearing the series of jewelled and enamelled pieces which he made for Calouste Gulbenkian, and the same disregard for function characterises all his work, and much of the other French work of the period. Even successful commercial firms like Boucheron or Vever are sometimes betrayed into flamboyance, though their's are among the more practical and wearable pieces in this style. On a different level Piel Frères, who made the plated buckle in the form of a girl with a harp (Plate 30), fully expected their pieces to be worn, and even possibly later discarded, since they hardly ever used either precious materials or complex techniques. The few English firms who looked to French Art-Nouveau for their inspiration found a compromise solution, and, while using the linear forms which characterise the style they reduced the high relief and abandoned the fragile *plique-à-jour* enamel. The little pendants, brooches, buckles and horn combs by Liberty & Co., and Murrle, Bennett & Co., and the buckles and medallion brooches by William Comyns often bear the signs of frequent use.

Unlike Lalique's fragile *objets de vertu* (Plate 31) and the elaborate archaeological and neo-Gothic jewellery, these unpretentious pieces are more revealing about everyday life; in the same way, for example, as a cravat-pin, a brooch with a sentimental message, a set of fragile seed-pearl work, or a mourning locket, which conjure up their owners in a way that the other pieces do not. Here the Hull Grundy Gift is particularly rich, having a great variety of pieces in secondary or non-precious materials of types which only rarely survive. The collection of sentimental and mourning pieces provides an insight into the nineteenth century character which is usually only hinted at in public collections. Usually date and place of manufacture are a matter for an informed guess, and the likelihood of finding supporting external evidence can generally be discounted. Here, on the other hand, the group of this type of material is so, comparatively speaking, large that a definite pattern of evidence begins to emerge. To give one example, amongst the collection of pieces of botanical and naturalistic jewellery which form the special groups known as the 'gardens', there are one or two with dated inscriptions, often giving a rather different picture from that provided by the 'informed guess'. Even more rare and as valuable to the student of jewellery history is the survival of a number of original cases which are often labelled so fully (with addresses or the records of medals and other awards) that the piece so cased can be dated within a very small span of years, sometimes as little as five or six. It is of course important to determine whether the case in question is actually that of the manufacturer or just of the retailer, but this is often simply a matter of research in directories and other records of the period.

Most of the botanical jewellery of the Romantic period has a specific message. The language of flowers – a complex system of meanings attached to different flower species by which a bunch of carefully selected flowers could convey a message – was used as a half-secret code in the early nineteenth century, and the blooms most frequently used in botanical jewellery are those which convey a message of affection or love. It would be naïve to assume that we can now read those messages without a key to the code; for instance, forget-me-not brooches would seem to have an easily translatable significance, but the forget-me-not flower in fact meant 'true love' and the plea not to forget was conveyed by mouse-eared-scorpion-grass! Other flowers which occur frequently as jewels in the first half of the nineteenth century are Pink Convolvulus, which means 'worth sustained by judicious and tender affection'; the rose, which has various meanings, among them 'happy love'; the sheaf of corn (most common in carved ivory) which means 'riches'; daisy, for 'I share your sentiments'; heart's-ease or pansy for 'you occupy my thoughts', sometimes rendered as 'pensées', a pun on the sound of the name; and ivy, which means either 'friendship' or 'fidelity' or even 'marriage'. One of Anne Hull Grundy's 'gardens', featured on the covers here, contains two branches of currants, made of gold and white chalcedony, a very much more uncommon design meaning 'you please all'. It is rather odd that the daffodil is not used; its meaning is 'regard' and it would seem to be quite as useful as any of the other much-used species, but this may be explained by the prevalence of 'regard' jewels where the message is conveyed by a special arrangement of stones – ruby, emerald, garnet, amethyst, ruby, diamond – the initial letters of each spelling the word. In some instances where the form of the jewel does not have any very obvious derivation, but combines flowers or leaves and insects, it is possible that some message of personal significance to the donor and recipient is intended.

The small group of jewelled cross-pendants dating from the late eighteenth and early nineteenth centuries are a poignant reminder of Jane Austen's pleasure at being given just such a pendant by her sailor brother, Charles. She writes, 'Of what avail is it to take prizes if he lays out the produce on presents to his sisters? He has been buying gold chains and topaze crosses for us – he must be well scolded'. (*Letters* 27 May, 1801). Lady Caroline Lamb received a number of jewelled crosses as wedding gifts in 1805, for instance, a topaz cross like Jane Austen's from her cousin Harriet Cavendish, and a pearl cross with a diamond in the centre from Lady Elizabeth Foster. Perhaps this was the one she wore when Lady Cowper saw her at a ball at Hatfield House many years later 'with her white cross, and a dirty gown as if she had been rolled in a kennel'.

The collection also includes another group of jewellery of rather similar pretensions to the sentimental or mourning pieces, but of a somewhat different character, the 'toys', charms and novelties of ingenious manufacture, often of coloured gold, a complex technique much used by box-makers in the eighteenth century, set with turquoises and other precious stones, which were very popular during the nineteenth century. Most of these pieces have an ostensible function as tiny containers, they could in theory have been used as vinaigrettes, and some even have the characteristic pierced inner lid which is found in a vinaigrette and used to confine the scent-soaked sponge, but release the perfume.

Many of these pieces have a message, often humorous in intention and presented in the form of a visual riddle like the stick pin with the head in the form of a bee on a cross with the letters DONT at the end of each arm, which, of course, reads 'DON'T BE CROSS'! The mice in their cage are labelled 'NOT FOR JOSEPH', a message so cryptic that it must have a purely personal significance.

There are even three pieces here which were literally toys, three bracelets for dolls, probably for the elaborately dressed 'mannequin' dolls which were used to display fashions before human models were employed. These are not gimcrack trash but real miniature jewellery made of gold and set with real stones or carefully enamelled. The tiny snake bracelet is an exact miniature of a very popular and fashionable type, the flexible links carefully overlapped in the same way as the full-sized original. These pieces being bracelets are easy to identify as dolls' jewellery, but other very minute brooches and buckles are less easy to distinguish from jewellery intended for babies and young children. There is a long tradition of bedecking children in ornaments which are merely scaled-down versions of their parents' jewels dating from at least the Renaissance when small white and black enamelled pendants, mainly of animals, were made in Florence for children, but some of the very fragile sprays seem to be hardly suitable even for the strictly confined eighteenth century child.

Throughout the nineteenth century there is a sense of some secret rear-guard battle being fought between the conflicting demands on the jewellery trade of large-scale production – to be achieved by some means or other whether by mechanisation or the employment of a great many underpaid workers, many of them women – and the maintenance of the highest possible technical standards. This was a period of widespread technical innovation, partly designed to absorb certain necessary mechanical processes, and partly an attempt to preserve or revive ancient methods of enamelling or goldsmithing which had fallen into disuse in the trade during the late eighteenth century with the absorbtion in gem-cutting and setting. The revival of archaeological techniques required the most skilled hand working in methods which were only evolved after painstaking research and experimentation. The ways of texturing and colouring gold were equally the subject of endless experiment with mixtures of alloy and acid-reaction. Those who succeeded in their experiments were in possession of valuable secrets which their trade rivals were always anxious to wrest from them by fair means or foul. Henri Vever recounts a long episode in the history of the Maison Robin, when they were anxious at some time in the 1840s to learn the well-kept English secret of how to 'bloom' gold to give a matt texture without losing the beautiful yellow colour of the metal. One of Robin's workmen was sent to England to do some spying. Money changed hands and English jewellers' employees were made drunk before the French firm could imitate this very fashionable English technique, but they seem to have yielded up their secret too late, and little use of this hard-won knowledge seems to have been made by the French.

The picture presented by the Hull Grundy Gift has its own significance in the history of taste. The emphasis throughout is on the study of the artist, the designer, the goldsmith and the craftsman creating and supplying the demands of fashion – in effect, the jeweller's art.

Notes on the Colour Plates

I
Gold pendant set with table-cut emeralds. Made in
two sections: the upper part is of purely decorative
form, whereas the design of the lower part incorporates
the 'S' impaled with a nail (to denote membership of a
religious confraternity).
 The back of the pendant is decorated with enamelled
colours painted on the white enamel ground. Spanish,
about 1640. W. 8·7 cm.

II
Pendant cylindrical cross, set with polished hardstones
in gold. Probably by Neuber of Dresden. German,
about 1770. L. 10 cm.
 Painted enamel portrait of Sidney Godolphin
(1645–1712), signed by Charles Boit, (set inside the lid
of a tortoiseshell *piqué-point* box), after a painting by
Kneller depicting the sitter in Garter robes (installed
K.G. in 1704). English, early 18th century. H. 8·2 cm.
 Blonde tortoiseshell box; decorated with gold *piqué-
point*. French, early 18th century. W. 8·2 cm.

III
Diamond and painted enamel Badge of the Anti-
Gallican Society, the central enamel showing St George
on horseback piercing with his spear a shield bearing
the three fleur-de-lis of France. The supporters are the
lion rampant of England on the left, and the double-
headed eagle of the Holy Roman Empire on the right.
Below, in a diamond-set pendant, is Britannia holding a
spear and a branch of laurel; above is an enamelled
ribbon with the motto 'For Our Country'. English,
mid-18th century. L. 14 cm.

IV 17th–18th Century Boxes
Ivory box, lid and sides carved and decorated with
applied gold animals, trees and the sun's rays to form
a landscape; the base carved and decorated with gold
piqué-point, including the fleur-de-lis. French,
late 17th century. W. 9 cm.
 Gold *ciselé* box. English, mid-18th century.
W. 6·5 cm.
 Gold *ciselé* box. English, about 1725–35. W. 7 cm.
 Gold and mother-of-pearl double miniature case,
with pierced trellis patterns, *piqué* and *ciselé* work.
French, early 18th century.
 **Late 17th–Early 18th Century
 Piqué and Tortoiseshell Boxes**
Box, set with inlays of mother-of-pearl and gold,
enriched with gold *piqué-point*. W. 7·8 cm.
 Oval box, decorated entirely in gold *piqué-point*
work. W. 8·2 cm.
 Oval box decorated with birds, insects and fruits
with strong oriental influence in the design. W. 7 cm.
 Box with chased silver and *piqué-point*. W. 7.5 cm.

**V French and English Coloured Gems
and Pastes, 17th–18th Centuries**
Arrow brooch set with diamonds and emeralds; the
arrow-head set with rubies; silver-gilt closed setting.
About 1670. L. 10·7 cm. Flower spray brooch, set with
red, green, yellow, blue and white pastes or crystals;
silver, closed-back setting. About 1760. W. 9·3 cm.
Flower-filled cornucopia brooch, set with red, green,
yellow and colourless pastes; silver, closed-back
setting, with applied gold wire ornament. About 1770.
W. 3·2 cm. Hairpin mount in the form of an opened
flower, set with green, yellow, blue, red and colourless
pastes; silver closed-back setting; the centre mounted
on a trembler spring. About 1770. D. 4·5 cm.

VI
Brooch, gold decorated with enamel in a relief
cloisonné technique of leaves and red and white
circles confined within borders of applied gold
wirework. The mosaic panel depicts the 'Lamb of God'
against a diapered ground. By Castellani of Rome.
Italian, about 1860. D. 5·3 cm.
 Brooch, of circular form flanked by two bulla-shaped
ornaments, gold repoussé work decorated with
wirework circles, having a mosaic panel with a Greek
inscription, surrounded by a border of fruiting vine,
the images bordered with gold *cloisons* (possibly
designed to imitate the appearance of cloisonné
enamel). By Castellani of Rome. Italian, about 1860.
W. 5·3 cms.

VII
Fringe necklace, plaited gold flexible chain with
seventeen mosaic-work pendants, neo-classical figures
in the 'Pompeiian' style, made by G. Roccheggiani of
Rome. Italian, about 1855. Central pendant 5·1 cm.
drop, necklace L. 41·2 cm.

VIII French 'Etruscan' Jewellery
Gold necklace in the 'Etruscan' style, with five
pendants, painted enamels in the 'Pompeiian' style,
designed and made by Eugène Fontenay (1823–87),
the enamels by Eugène Richet (*fl.* from 1861), boxed
by Boucheron, 152 & 153 Galerie des Valois. French,
between 1867 and 1873. D. (of central pendant) 2·9 cm.

IX Italian 'Archaeological' Jewellery
Necklace and pendant, plaited gold, pendant in the
form of a haloed 'Greek' cross, set with a carbuncle
(cabochon garnet), marked on the reverse FIORENTINI.
Italian, about 1870. Pendant 6·9 cm. drop. Brooch-
pendant, enamelled gold in the 'Etruscan' style set with
a sard intaglio signed with the Greek characters for
SKYL, possibly by the same maker as the necklace.
Italian, about 1870. 6·4 cm. drop.

X Italian Cameo Jewellery
Top row: Pendant, onyx cameo, female portrait bust,
attributed to T. Saulini, gold setting by Castellani.
About 1860. L. 6.5 cm. Brooch, onyx cameo,
helmetted female warrior, attributed to L. Saulini,
enamelled gold setting probably by Carlo Doria.
About 1870. L. 7 cm. Pendant, onyx cameo, classical
female bust, gold setting by Pierret. About 1870.
L. 6·6 cm.
Middle row: Brooch, onyx cameo, portrait of Dante,
attributed to L. Saulini, enamelled gold setting by
Castellani. About 1860. D. 4·2 cm. Pendant, onyx
cameo helmetted female warrior, attributed to
L. Saulini in a jewelled and enamelled gold setting
possibly by Civilotti. About 1860. L. 7·2 cm.

Bottom row: Brooch, onyx cameo, female portrait bust signed 'L. Saulini F.', enamelled silver-gilt setting possibly by Carlo Doria. About 1860. L. 5·4 cm. Brooch, shell cameo of 'Aurora driving her biga' signed 'Saulini', enamelled gold setting probably by Carlo Doria. About 1860. W. 5·9 cm. Brooch, shell cameo, 'Roma', Saulini workshop, gold setting by Carlo Doria. 1862. L. 5·5 cm.

XI Italian Cameo Jewellery
Top row: Pendant, onyx cameo of George III by Pistrucci. About 1816. L. 4·1 cm. Brooch, chalcedony cameo of a helmetted warrior's head signed 'Catenacci'. About 1840. W. 4·2 cm. Pendant, onyx cameo, bust of Bacchus, signed 'Morelli'. About 1820. L. 4·2 cm.
Middle row: Brooch, onyx cameo, bust of Bacchus, signed 'Girometti'. About 1835. L. 3·7 cm. Brooch, onyx cameo of a helmetted female warrior (Cleopatra?), signed 'Girometti' in an enamelled gold setting. About 1840. L. 6·4 cm. Brooch, onyx cameo, head of a girl, signed in Greek characters, Rega. About 1810. L. 3·1 cm.
Bottom row: Brooch, portrait bust of Admiral Lord Nelson, signed in Greek characters, Rega. About 1800. 4 cm. Brooch, agate cameo portrait bust, signed 'Berini'. About 1820. L. 5·1 cm. Brooch, onyx cameo, classical male head, signed 'Berini'. About 1820. L. 4·7 cm.

XII Castellani and Giuliano
Top: Bracelet, one of a pair, with chalcedony cameos of six Roman emperors alternating with square links set with cabochon rubies and emeralds. By Castellani. Italian, about 1870. L. 22·1 cm.
Lower: Necklace, gold with coral cameo pendants. By Carlo Giuliano. English, about 1860. L. (of centre cameo) 2·7 cm. Cruciform pendant, enamelled gold set with pearls. By Carlo Giuliano. English, about 1880. W. 3·8 cm.

Pectoral cross and chain, gold, neo-gothic style pierced with the words PER CRUCEM AD LUCEM set with a ruby, emeralds and sapphires. By William Burges. English, about 1860. L. 9·3 cm.

XIII French Neo-Gothic Jewellery
Brooch, in the form of a trefoil with a dragon. By Jules Wièse. About 1860. H. 3·9 cm. Pendant, enamelled gold head of the Virgin in a quatrefoil frame. By Jules Wièse. About 1860. H. 4·2 cm. Pendant and chain, oxidized silver and gold, inserted blue glass panels. By F. D. Froment-Meurice. About 1850. W. (of pendant) 6·1 cm.

XIV English Reversed Crystal Intaglios 1860–80
Top: Brooch, two pheasants in a landscape, backed with mother-of-pearl, in gold collet setting. W. 3·4 cm. Pair of brooches, cock and hen pheasants in reeds and grasses, set in gold mounts by John Brogden. 2·3 cm. square.
Middle: Brooch, head of a Pomeranian dog, backed with gold, on the reverse an inscription to 'MUFF obit Nov. 24th 1862 at Dinapore, Aged 8 years and 6 months', and a compartment containing hair, in a gold collet setting. D. 3·4 cm. Pendant, robin in a snowy landscape, backed with gold, the reverse with a compartment containing a tinted photograph of a bearded man in a gold locket case ornamented with twisted ropework and gold beads. L. 6·1 cm. drop. Brooch, bee with gold backing, the reverse set with a compartment for hair, in a gold mount ornamented with twisted ropework and beads. D. 3·1 cm.
Lower: Pair of earrings, crystal globes with goldfish set in a gold band. The three-dimensional effect is achieved by backing two mirror-image crystals and concealing the join in the gold band. In the original case labelled W. J. Thomas, Jeweller and Silversmith 136 Oxford Street, London. D. of globe, 1·9 cm. Brooch-pendant, tiger's head in a gold setting flanked by four tiger claws, marked on the reverse [JM]. W. 7·3 cm.

XV Japanese-style Coloured Gold Jewellery by Tiffany of New York
Fringe-necklace, gold chain ornamented with bead-work, with twenty-four open-work filigree pendants ornamented with flowers and exotic birds in four-colour gold-work. About 1870. L. 35·5 cm. Brooch, hammered-gold in the form of a Japanese fan, ornamented with leaves and a butterfly in three-colour gold-work, marked on the reverse with a monogram 'TCo'. About 1870. W. 3·9 cm. Demi-parure: shell-shaped brooch and earrings ornamented with a water-bird amongst reeds in four-colour gold-work. About 1880. Brooch, W. 6·6 cm., earrings, H. 2·4 cm.

Cloisonné enamel locket-pendant, with Japanese-style images of a cockerell and, on the reverse, a vase of flowers, marked 'AF' flanking a flail for Alexis Falize, (1811–98, retired 1876). French, about 1869. H. 5·4 cm.

XVI French Gold Art-Nouveau Jewellery
Double leopard buckle, cast glass lion's mask, made by Boucheron. One version was shown at the Paris Centennial Exposition in 1900. H. 7·8 cm. Winged dragon buckle in chased gold. About 1880. H. 6·9 cm. Two-colour gold buckle, draped female figure with a lion's mask. About 1905. H. 7·5 cm. *Plaque-de-cou,* chased gold leaves and pearl flowers. By Vever (?). About 1900. W. 7·7 cm.

Copenhagen Porcelain Waist-clasp
After a design by Georg Jensen. Danish, about 1902. W. 11·2 cm.

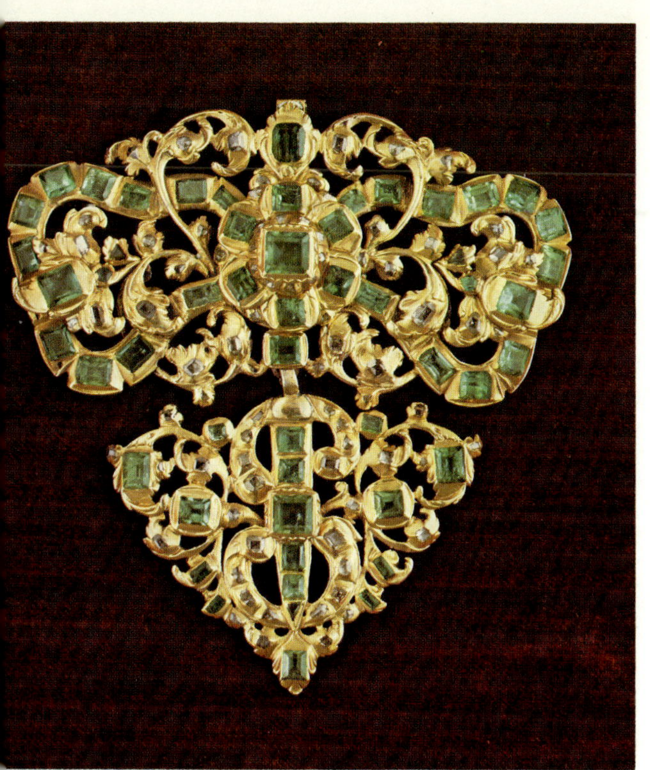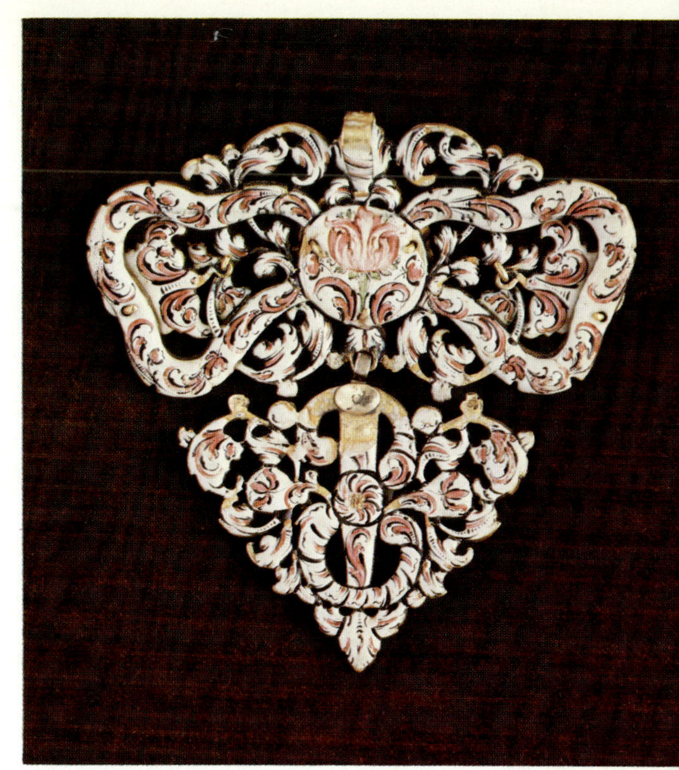

I

Gold pendant set with table-cut emeralds. The design of the lower part incorporates the 'S'
impaled with a nail (to denote membership of a religious confraternity). Spanish, about 1640.
W. 8·7 cm.

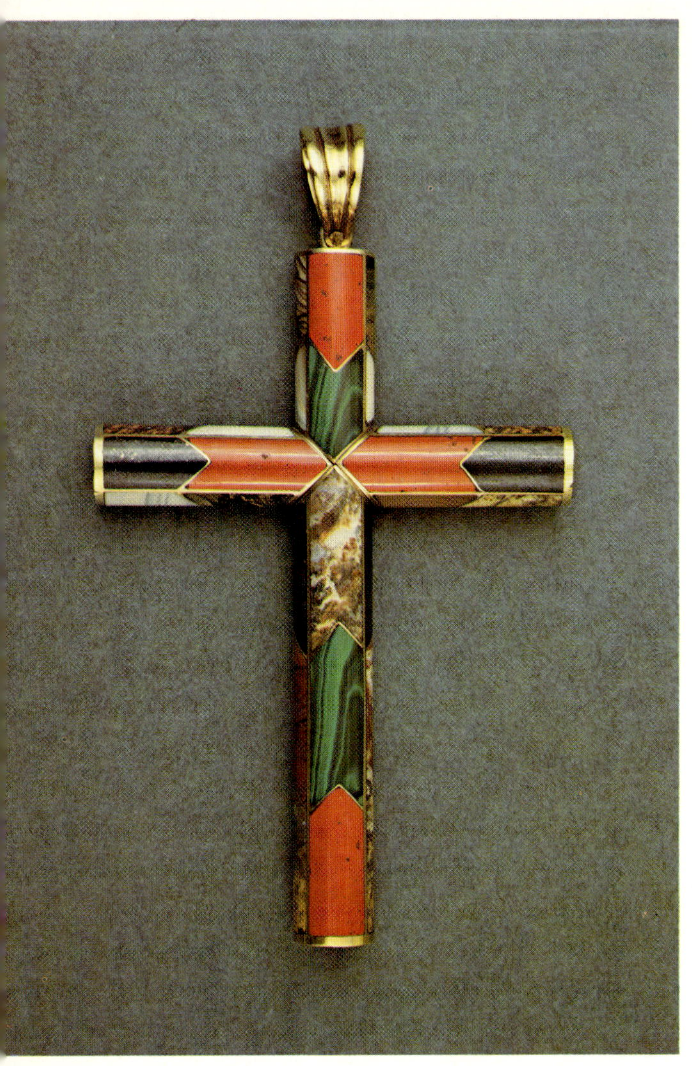

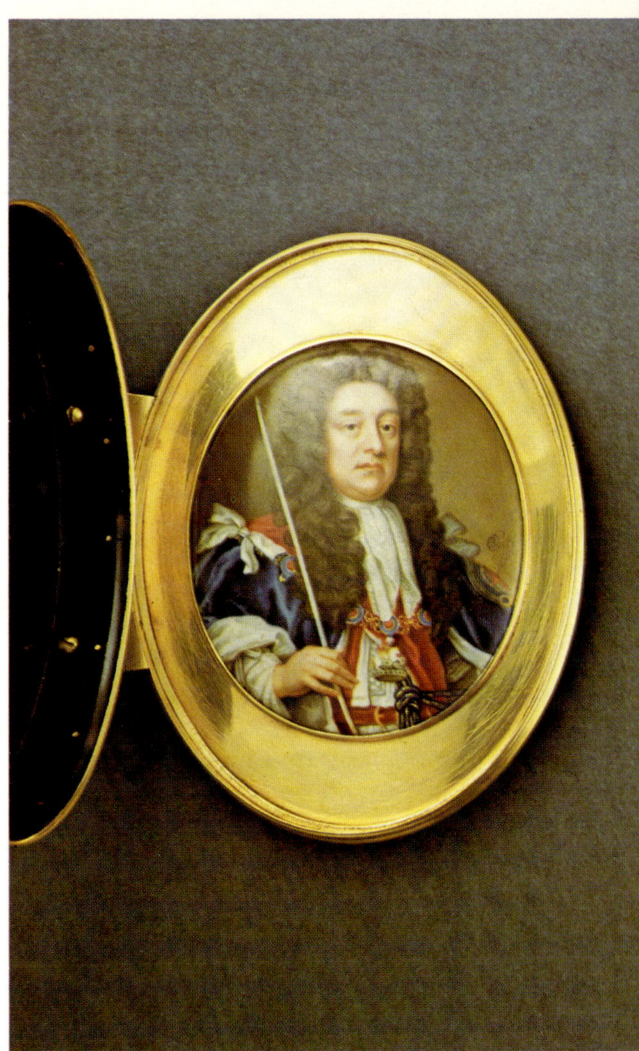

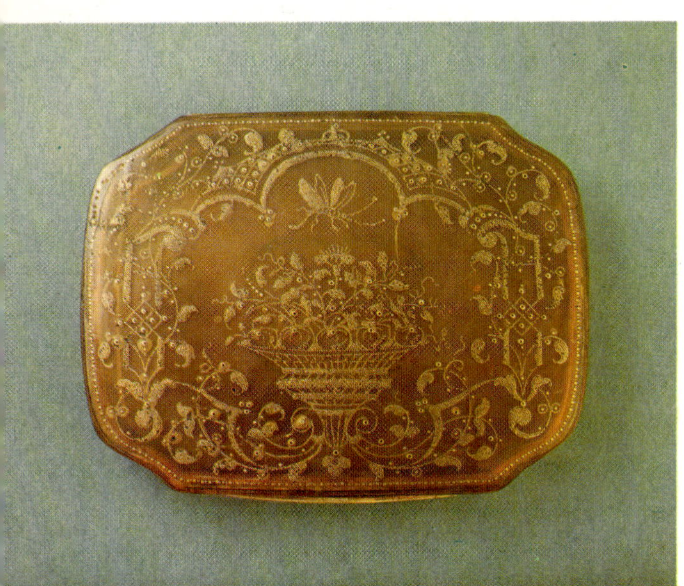

II

Pendant cylindrical cross, set with polished
hardstones in gold. Probably by Neuber of
Dresden. German, about 1770. L. 10 cm.

Painted enamel portrait of Sidney Godolphin
(1645–1712), signed by Charles Boit (set
inside the lid of a tortoiseshell *piqué-point* box).
English, early 18th century.

Blonde tortoiseshell box; decorated with gold
piqué-point. French, early 18th century.
W 8·2 cm.

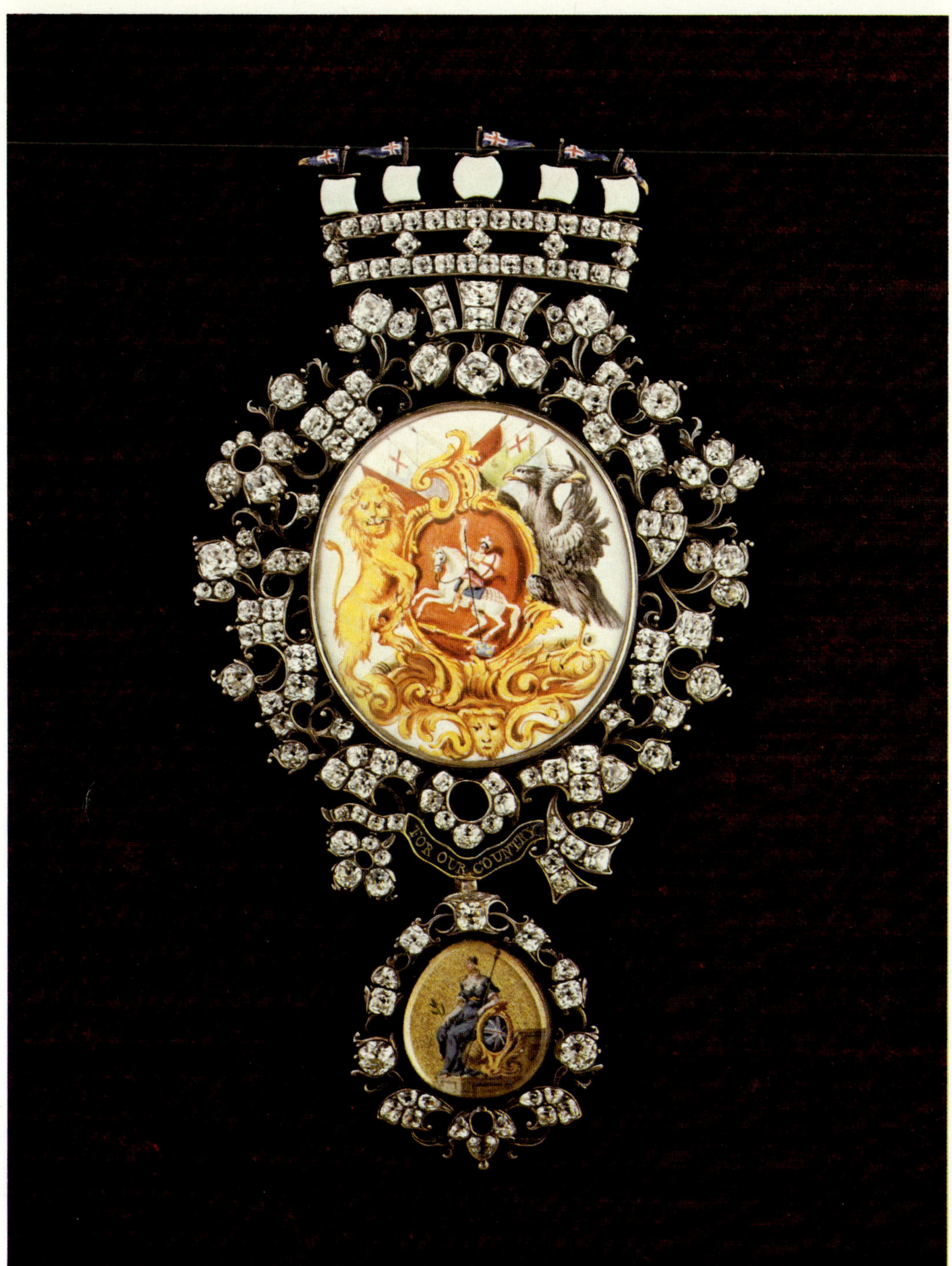

III

Diamond and painted enamel Badge of the Anti-Gallican Society, the central enamel showing
St George on horseback piercing with his spear a shield bearing the three fleurs-de-lis of
France. English, mid-18th century. L. 14 cm.

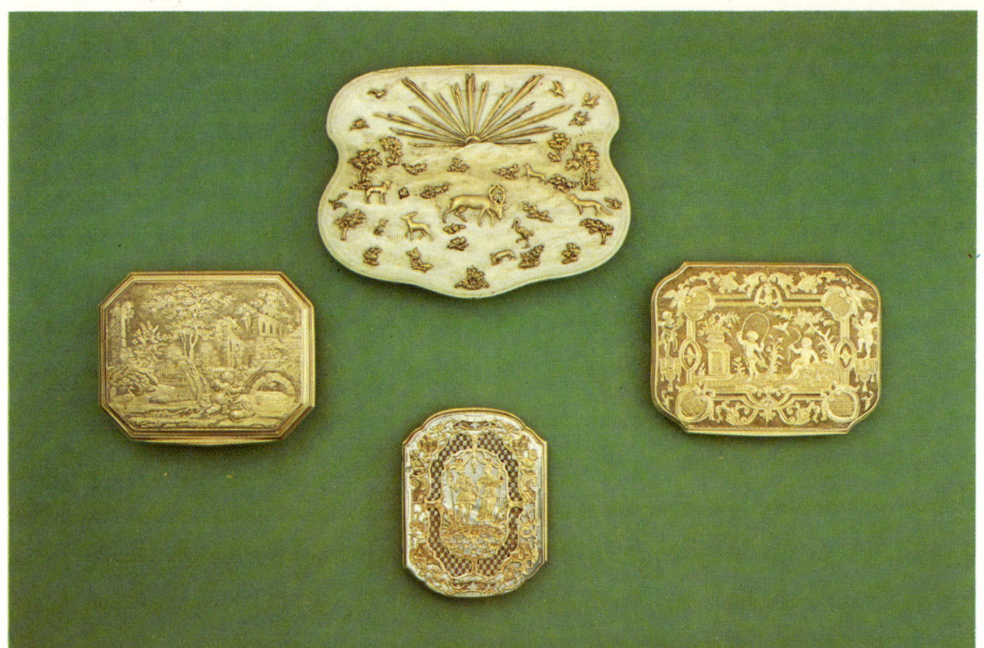

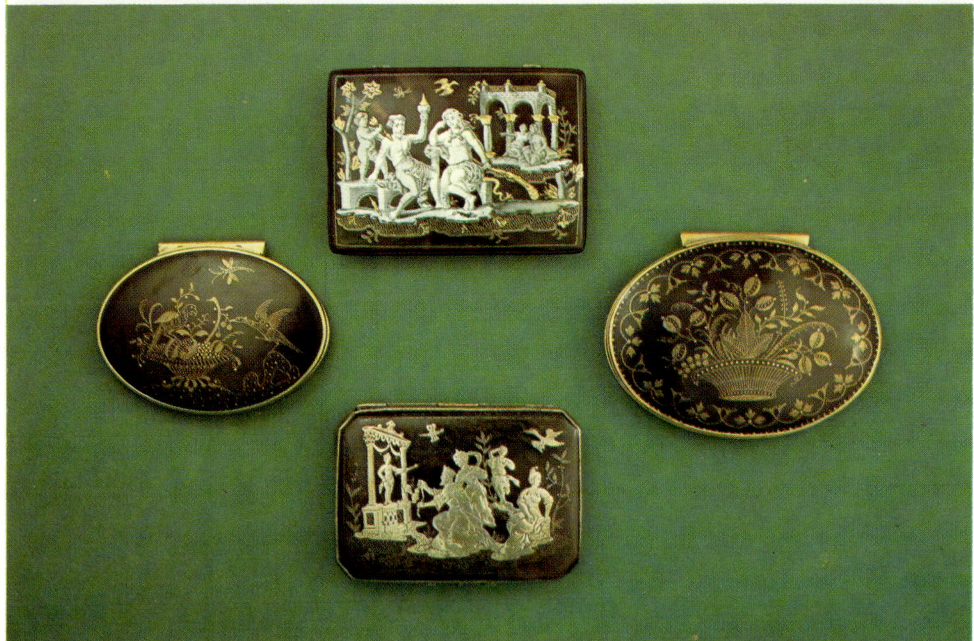

IV 17th–18th-century Boxes

Ivory box, lid and sides carved and decorated with applied motifs in gold. French, late
17th century. W. 9 cm. Gold ciselé box. English, mid-18th century. W. 6·5 cm. Gold ciselé
box. English, about 1725–35. W. 7 cm. Gold and mother-of-pearl double miniature case.
French, early 18th century.

Late 17th–early 18th-century Gold Piqué and Tortoiseshell Boxes

Box, set with inlays of mother-of-pearl and gold. W. 7·8 cm. Oval box, decorated entirely in
gold *piqué-point* work. W. 8·2 cm. Oval box decorated with birds, insects and fruits.
W. 7 cm. Box with chased silver and *piqué-point*. W. 7·5 cm.

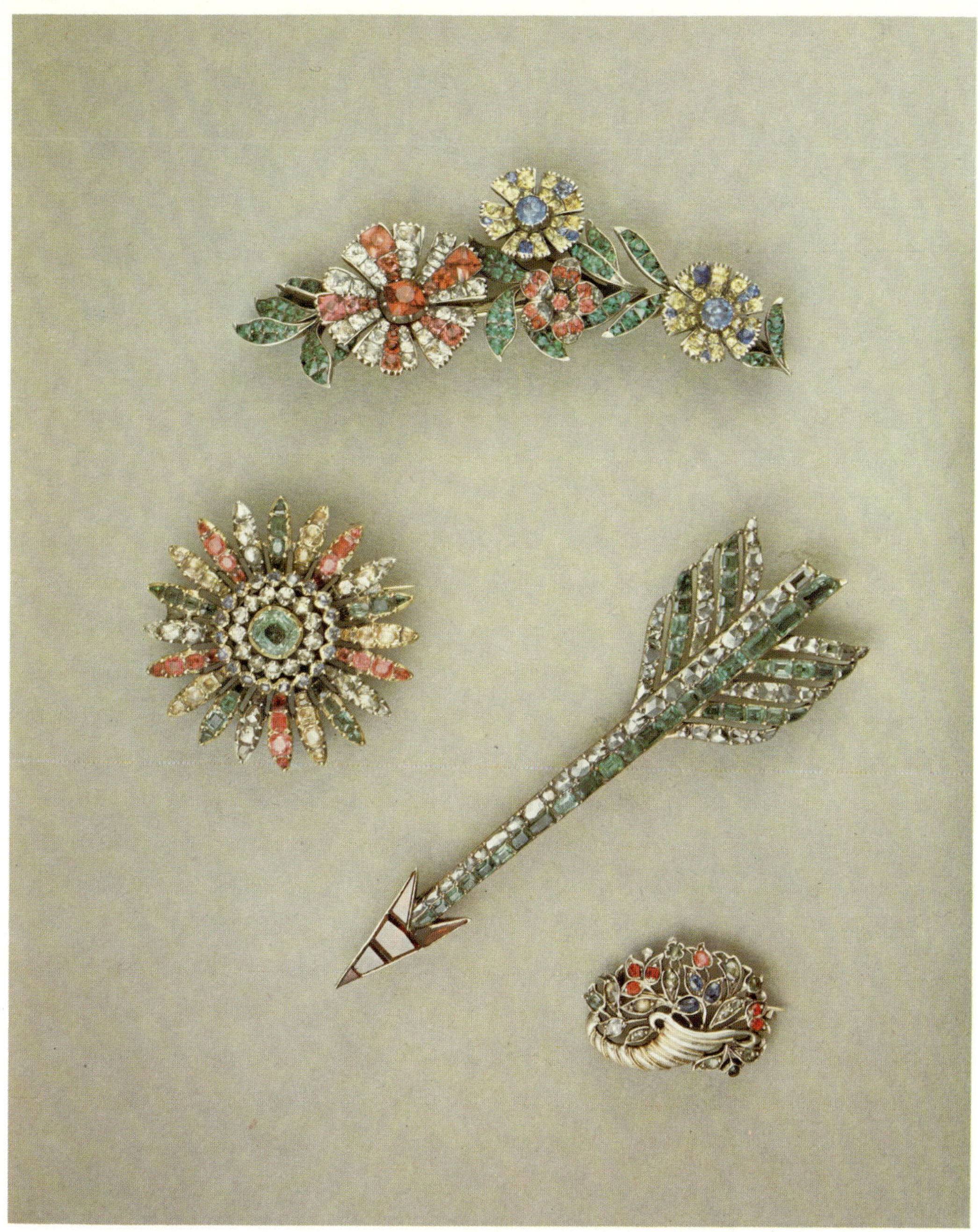

V French and English Coloured Gems and Pastes, 17th–18th centuries

Arrow brooch set with rubies, diamonds and emeralds. About 1670. L. 10·7 cm. Flower spray brooch, set with red, green, yellow, blue and white pastes or crystals. About 1760. W. 9·3 cm. Flower-filled cornucopia brooch, set with red, green, yellow and colourless pastes. About 1770. W. 3·2 cm. Hairpin mount in the form of an opened flower, set with green, yellow, blue, red and colourless pastes. About 1770. D. 4·5 cm.

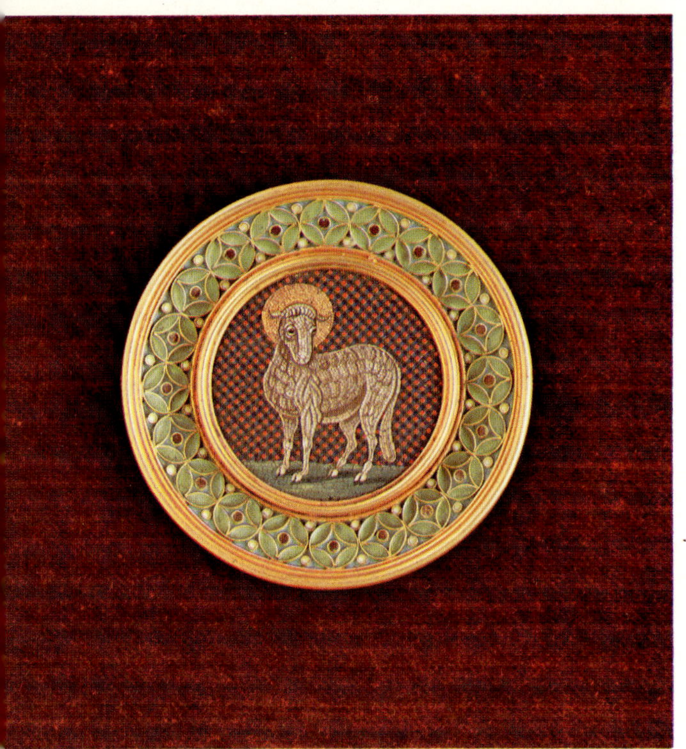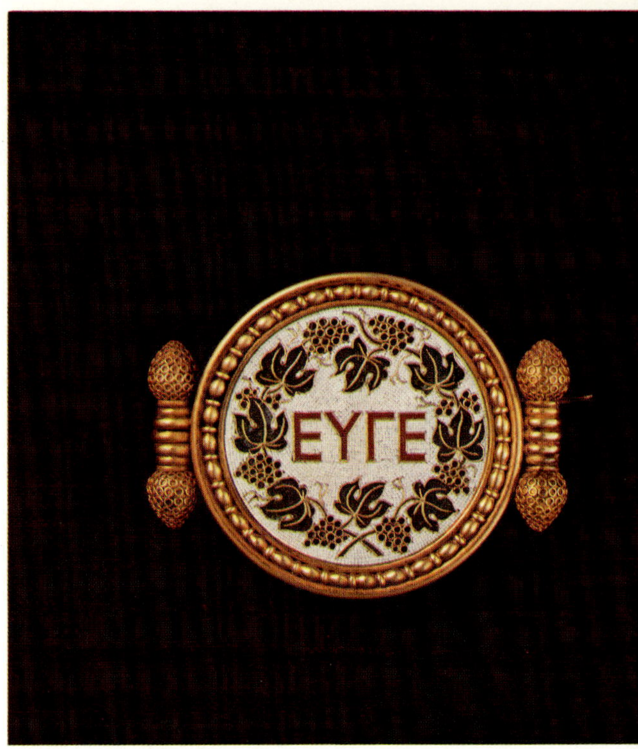

VI

Brooch, gold decorated with enamel in a relief cloisonné technique. The mosaic panel depicts the 'Lamb of God' against a diapered ground. By Castellani of Rome. Italian, about 1860. D. 5·3 cm.

Brooch, of circular form flanked by two bulla-shaped ornaments, having a mosaic panel with a Greek inscription. By Castellani of Rome. Italian, about 1860. W. 5·3 cm.

VII

Fringe necklace, plaited gold flexible chain with seventeen mosaic-work pendants in the 'Pompeiian' style. By G. Roccheggiani of Rome. Italian, about 1855. Central pendant 5·1 cm. drop, necklace L. 41·2 cm.

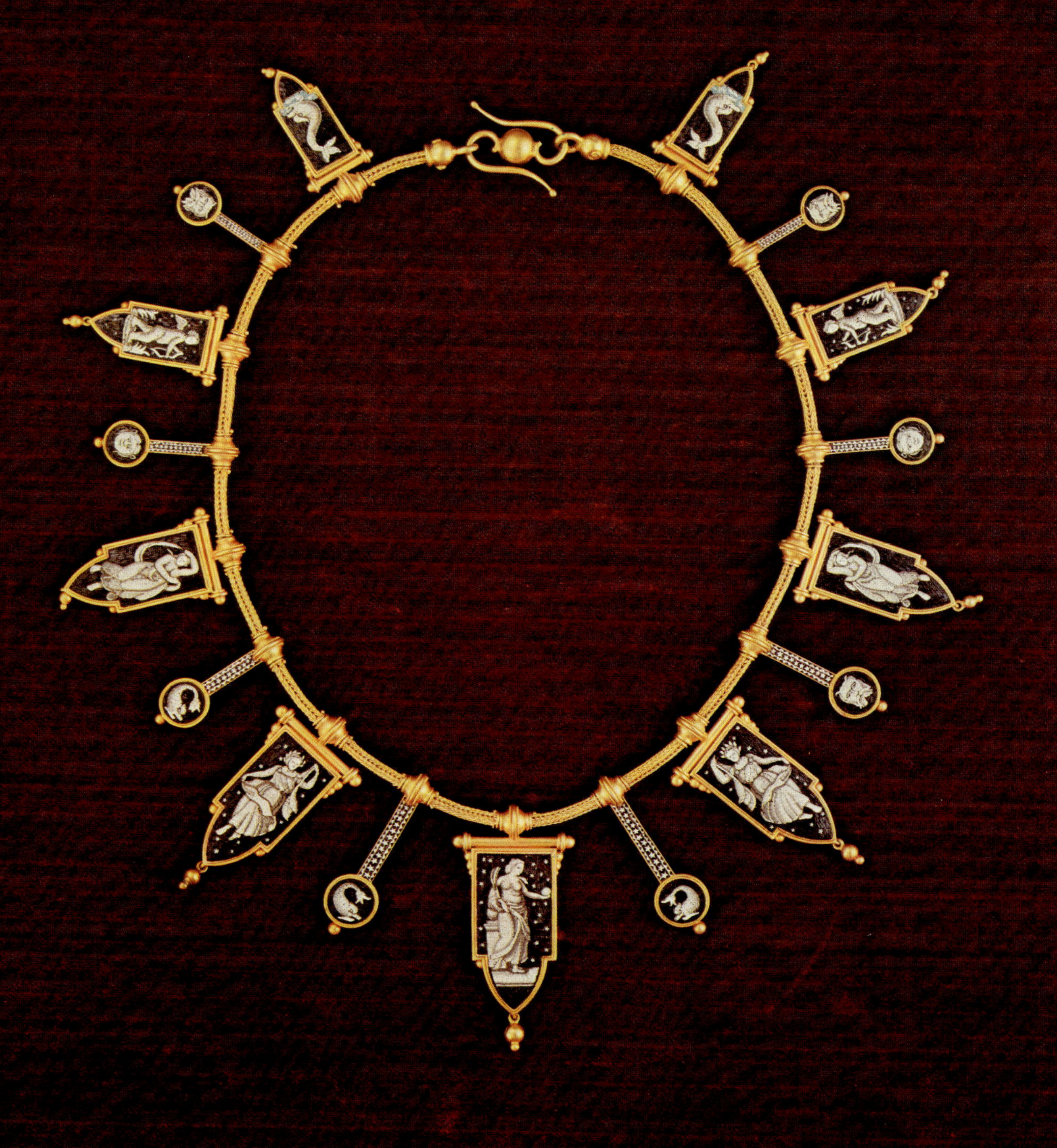

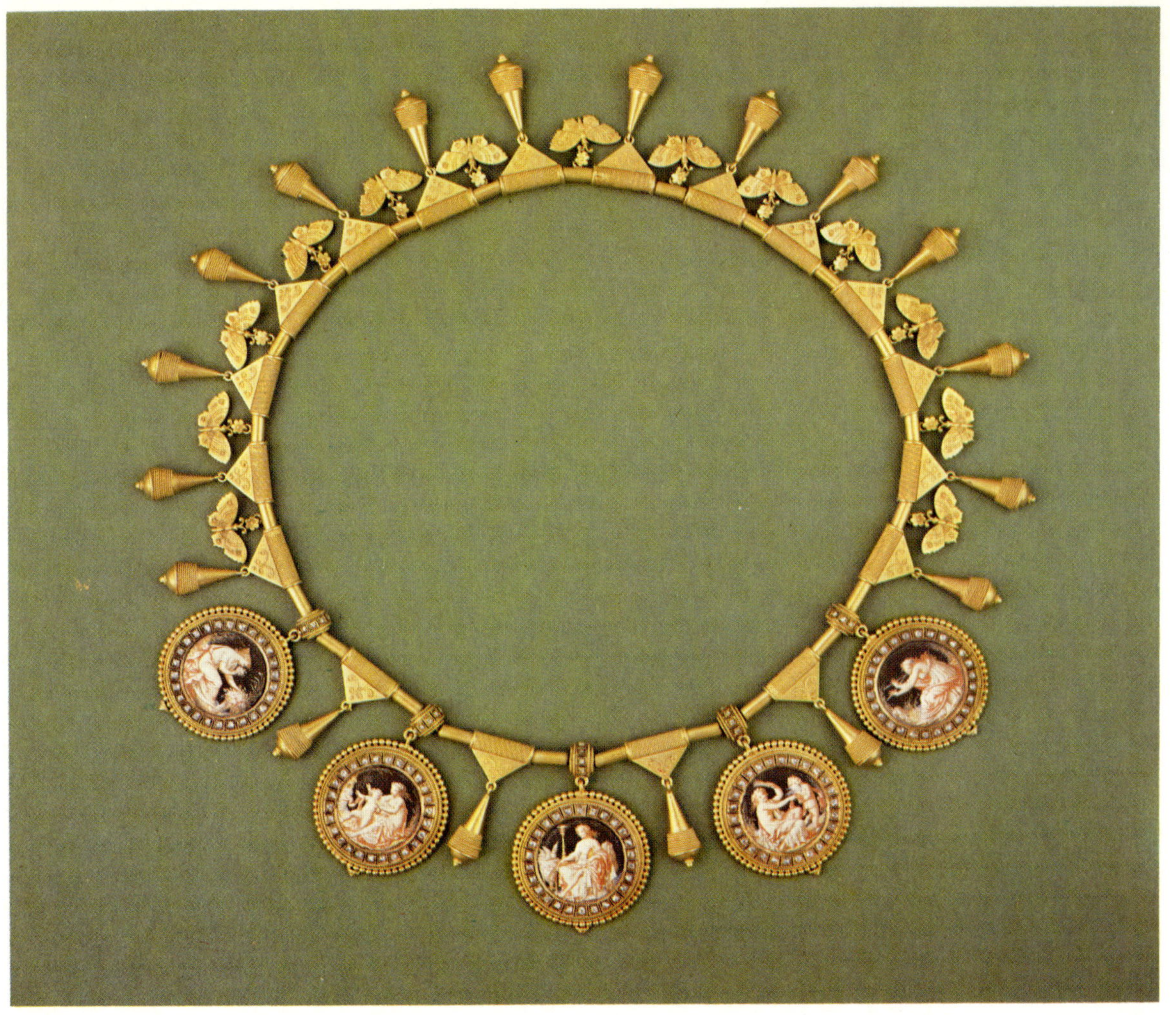

VIII French 'Etruscan' Jewellery

Gold necklace in the 'Etruscan' style, with five pendants in the 'Pompeiian' style, designed and made by Eugène Fontenay (1823–87). French, between 1867 and 1873. D. (of central pendant) 2·9 cm.

IX Italian 'Archaeological' Jewellery

Necklace and pendant, plaited gold, pendant in the form of a haloed 'Greek' cross. Italian, about 1870. Pendant 6·9 cm. drop. Brooch-pendant, enamelled gold in the 'Etruscan' style set with a sard intaglio signed with the Greek characters for SKYL. Italian, about 1870. 6·4 cm. drop.

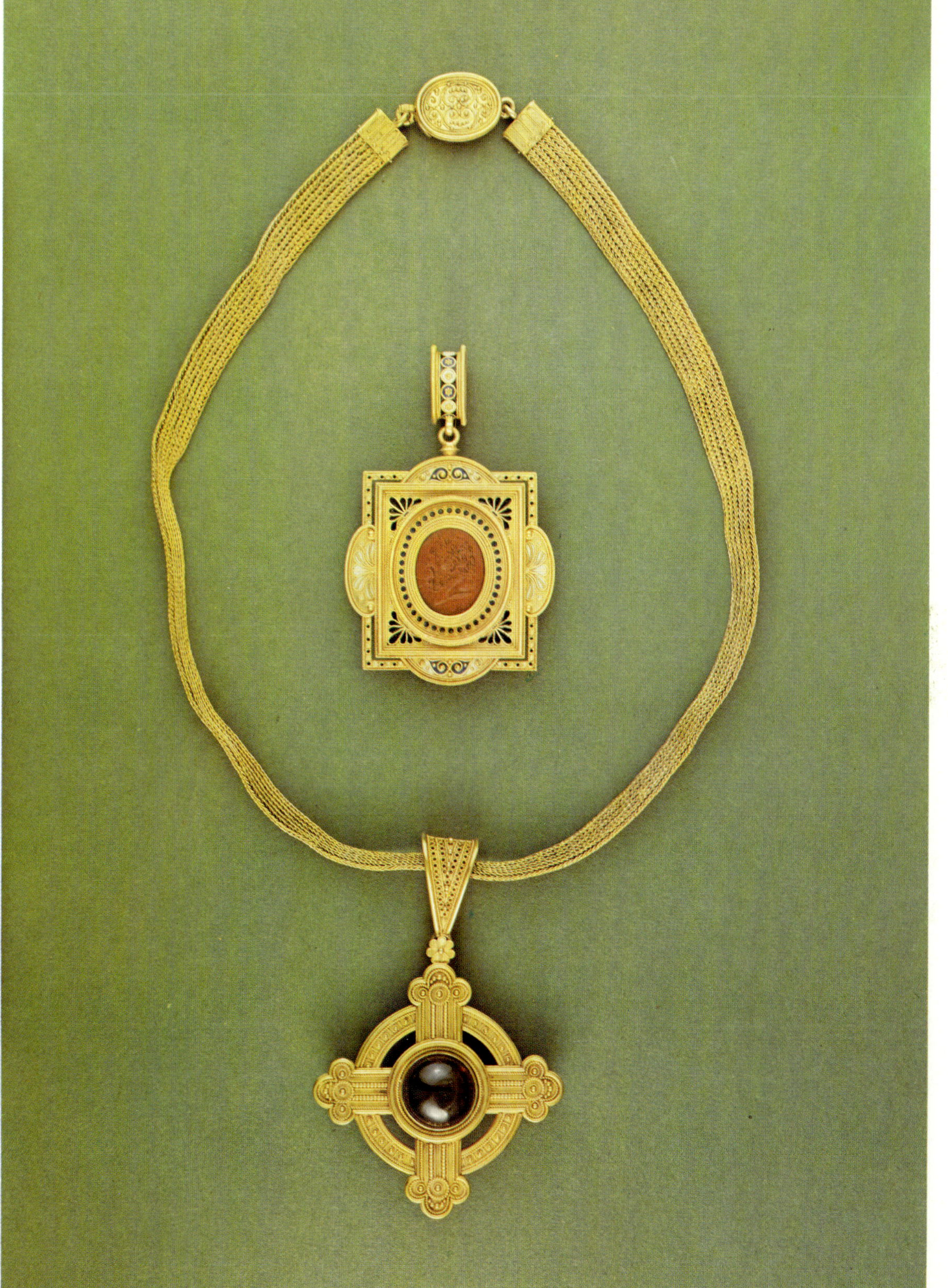

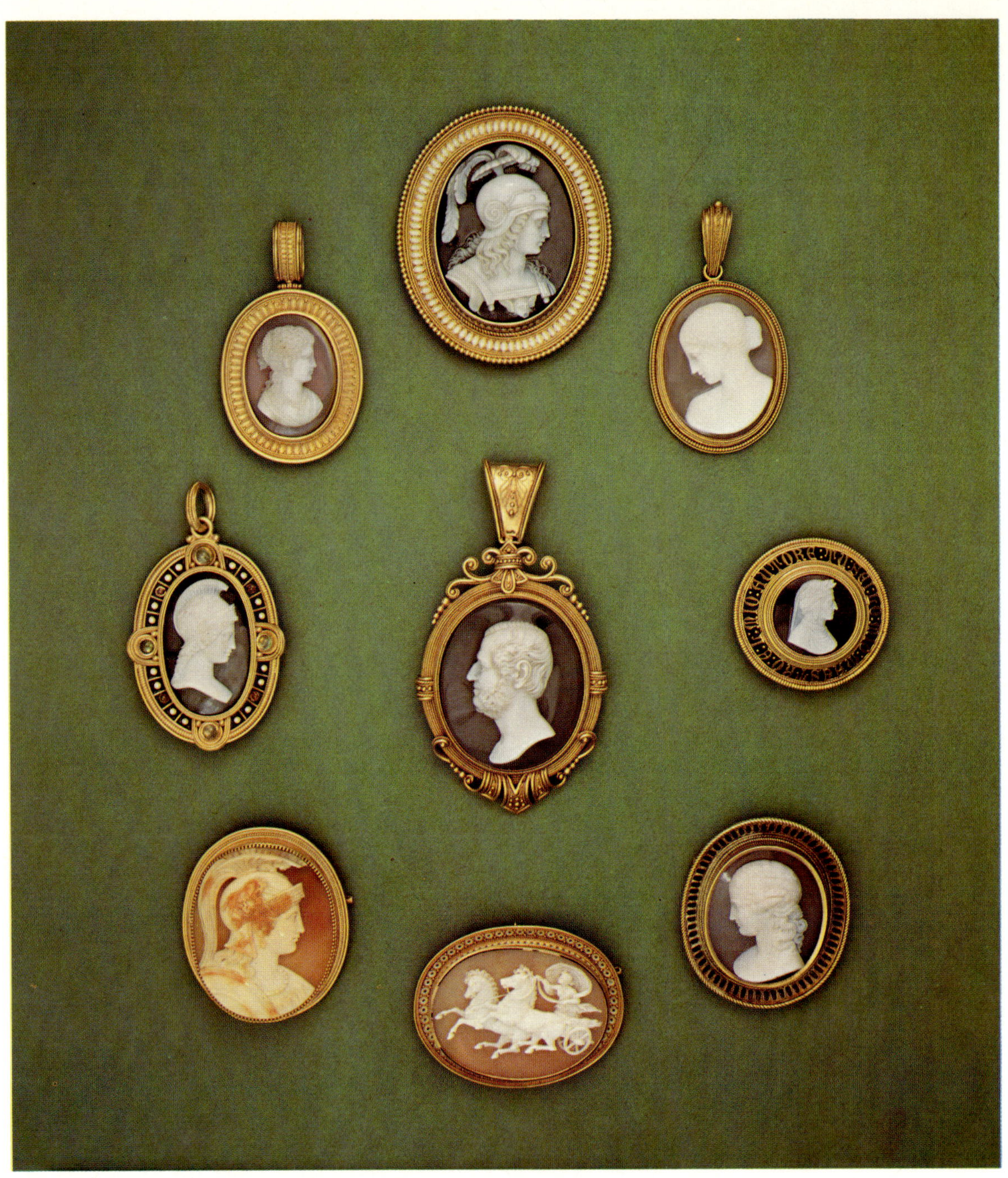

X Italian Cameo Jewellery, 1860–72

Mainly carved by Luigi Saulini with settings by Carlo Doria, Pierret and Civilotti. Largest piece, L. 7 cm.

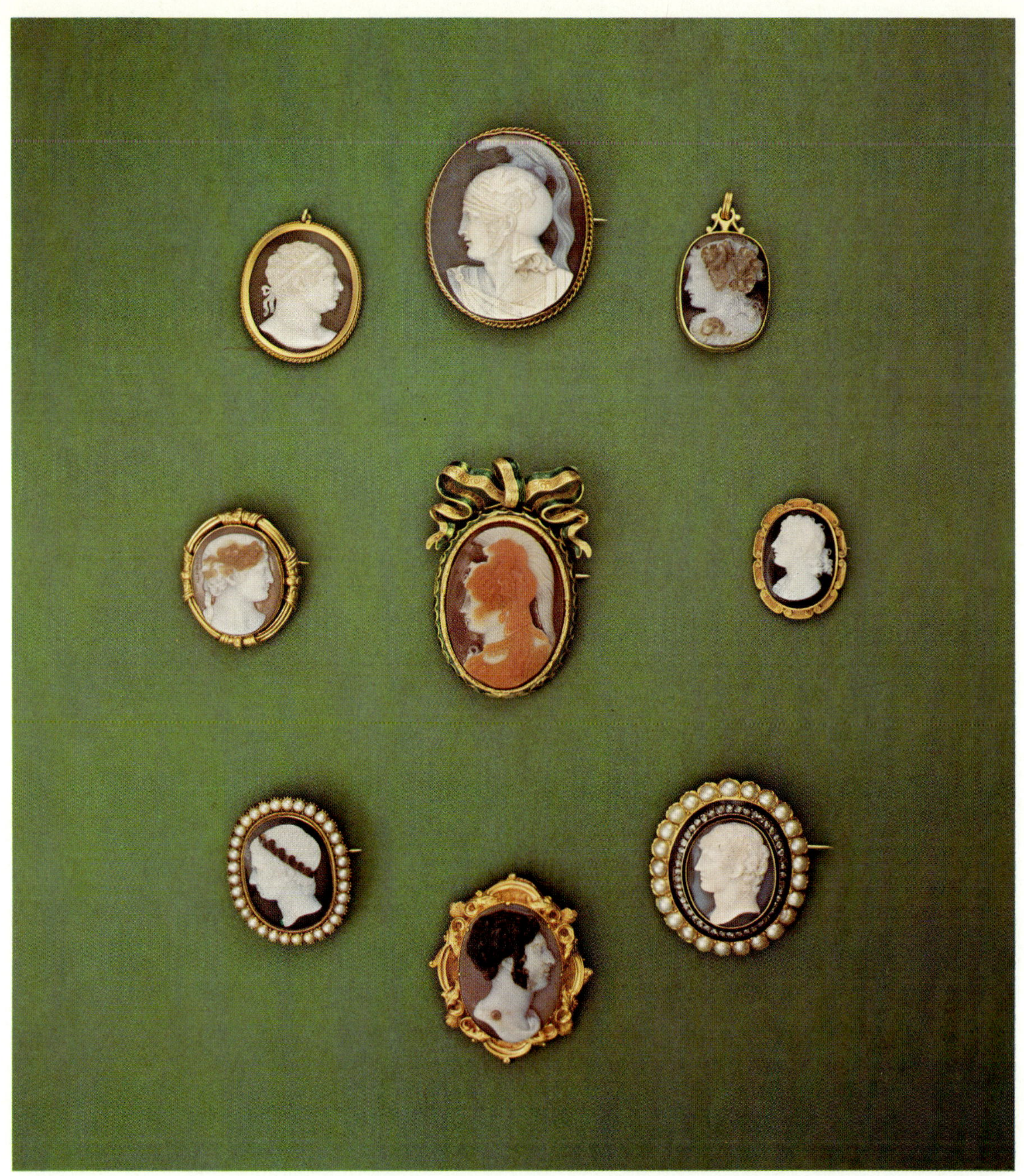

XI Italian Cameo Jewellery, 1810–40

Signed examples by Pistrucci, Catenacci, Morelli, Girometti, Rega, and Berini. Largest
piece, L. 6·4 cm.

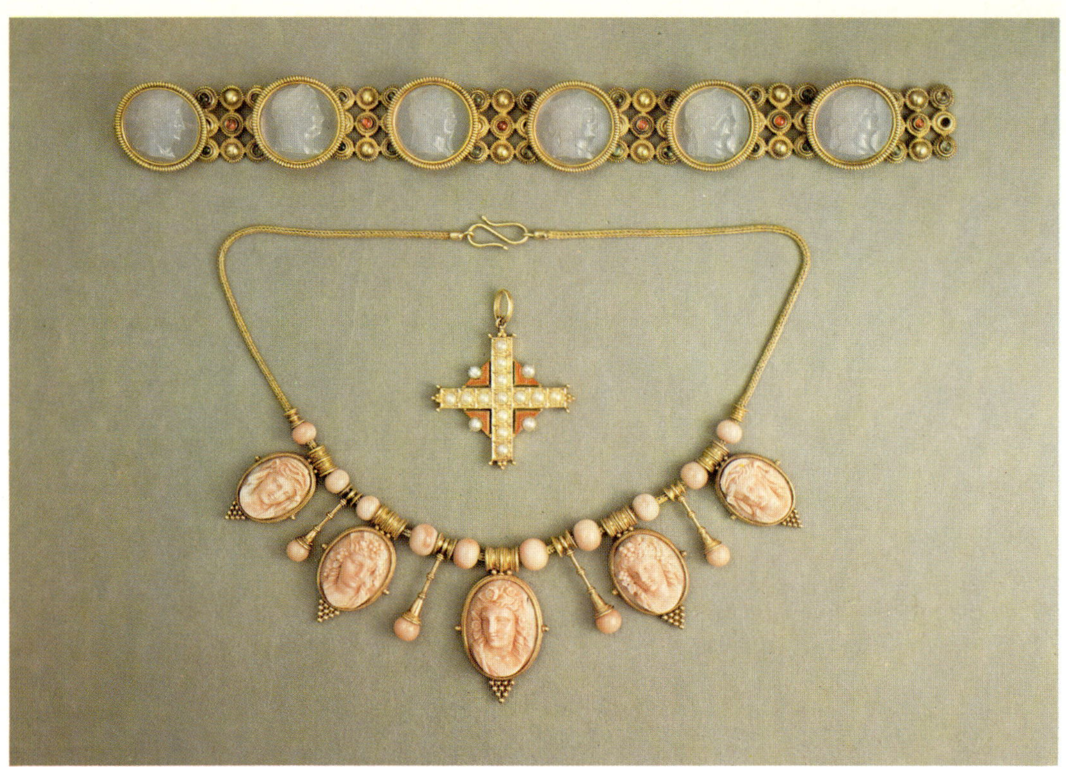

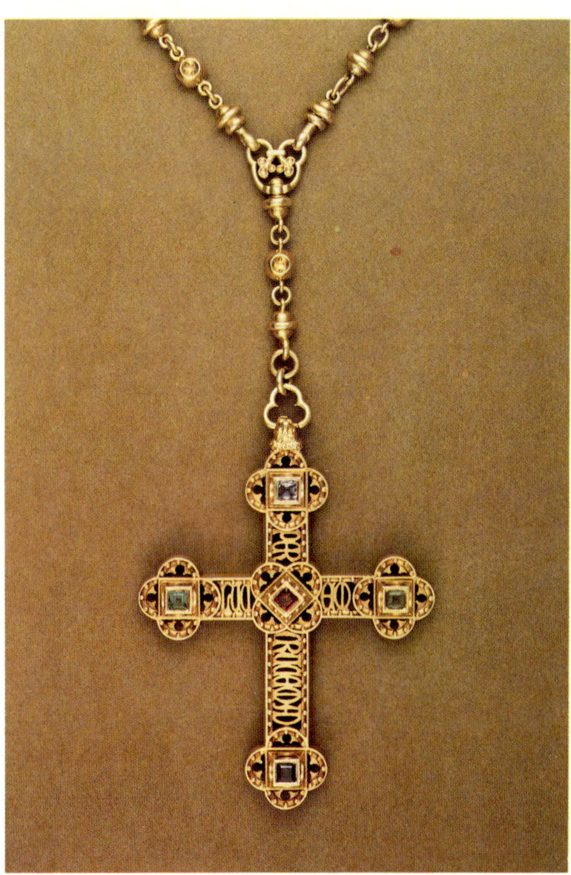

XII

Castellani and Giuliano
Bracelet, with chalcedony cameos of six
Roman emperors. By Castellani. Italian, about
1870. L. 22·1 cm. Necklace, gold with coral
cameo pendants. By Carlo Giuliano. English,
about 1860. L. (of centre cameo) 2·7 cm.
Cruciform pendant, enamelled gold set with
pearls. By Carlo Giuliano. English, about
1880. W. 3·8 cm.

Gold pectoral cross and chain. By William
Burges. English, about 1860. L. 9·3 cm.

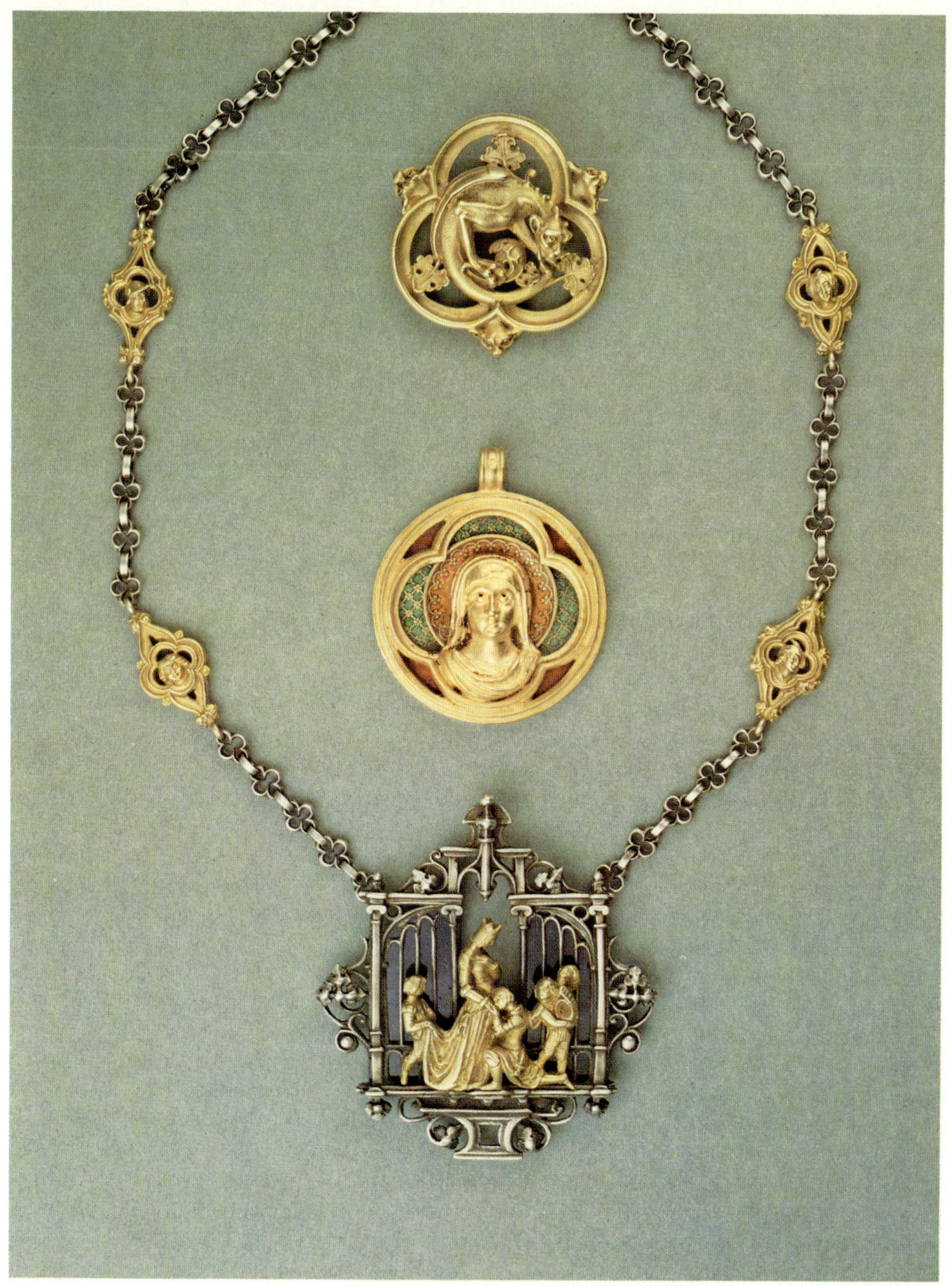

XIII French Neo-Gothic Jewellery

Brooch, in the form of a trefoil with a dragon. By Jules Wièse, about 1860. H. 3·9 cm.
Pendant, enamelled gold head of the Virgin in a quatrefoil frame. By Jules Wièse, about
1860. H. 4·2 cm. Pendant and chain, oxidized silver, gold, and glass. By F. D. Froment-
Meurice, about 1850. W. (of pendant) 6·1 cm.

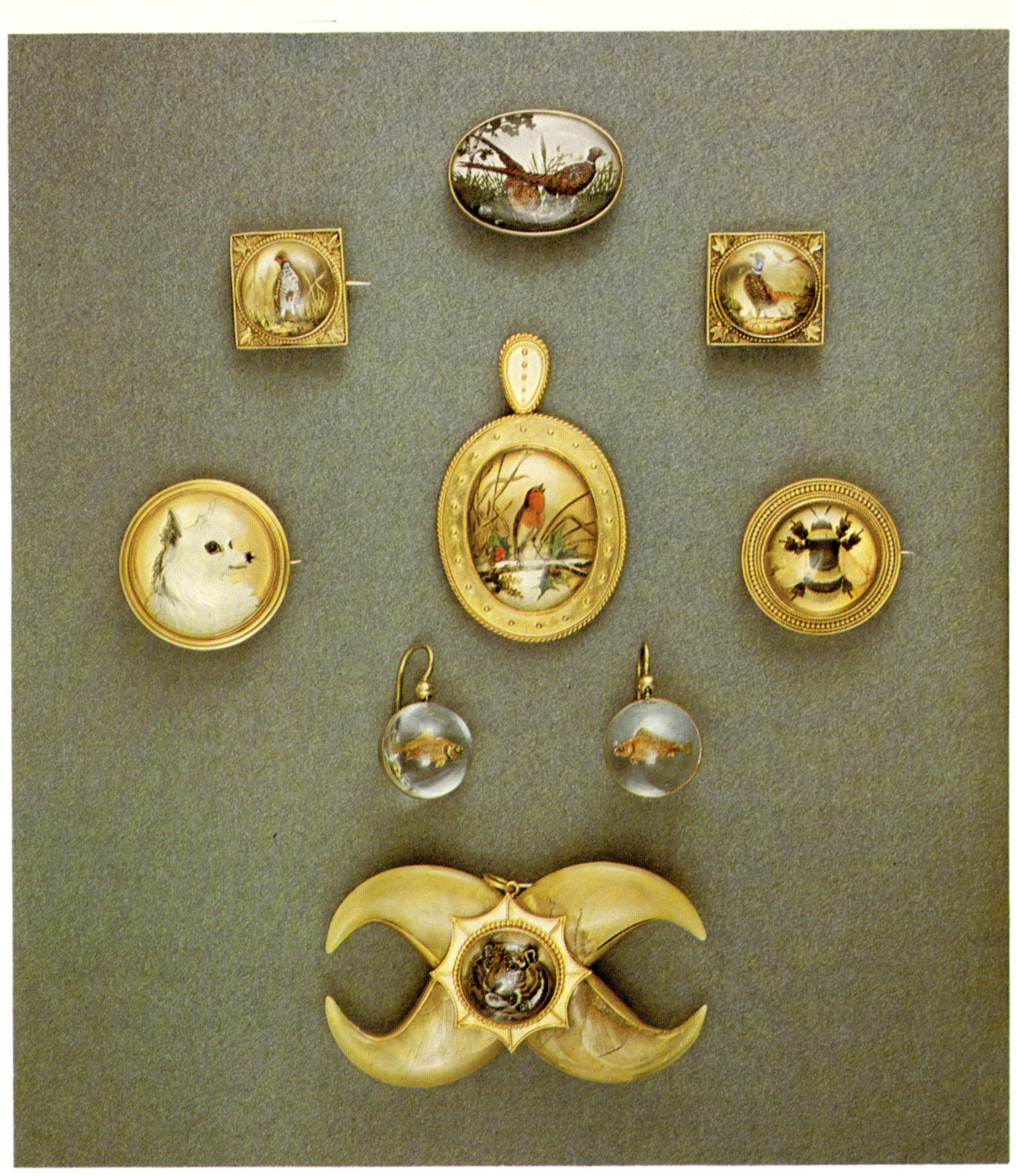

XIV English Reversed Crystal Intaglios with Gold Settings, 1860–80

Largest piece, brooch-pendant with tiger's head. W. 7·3 cm.

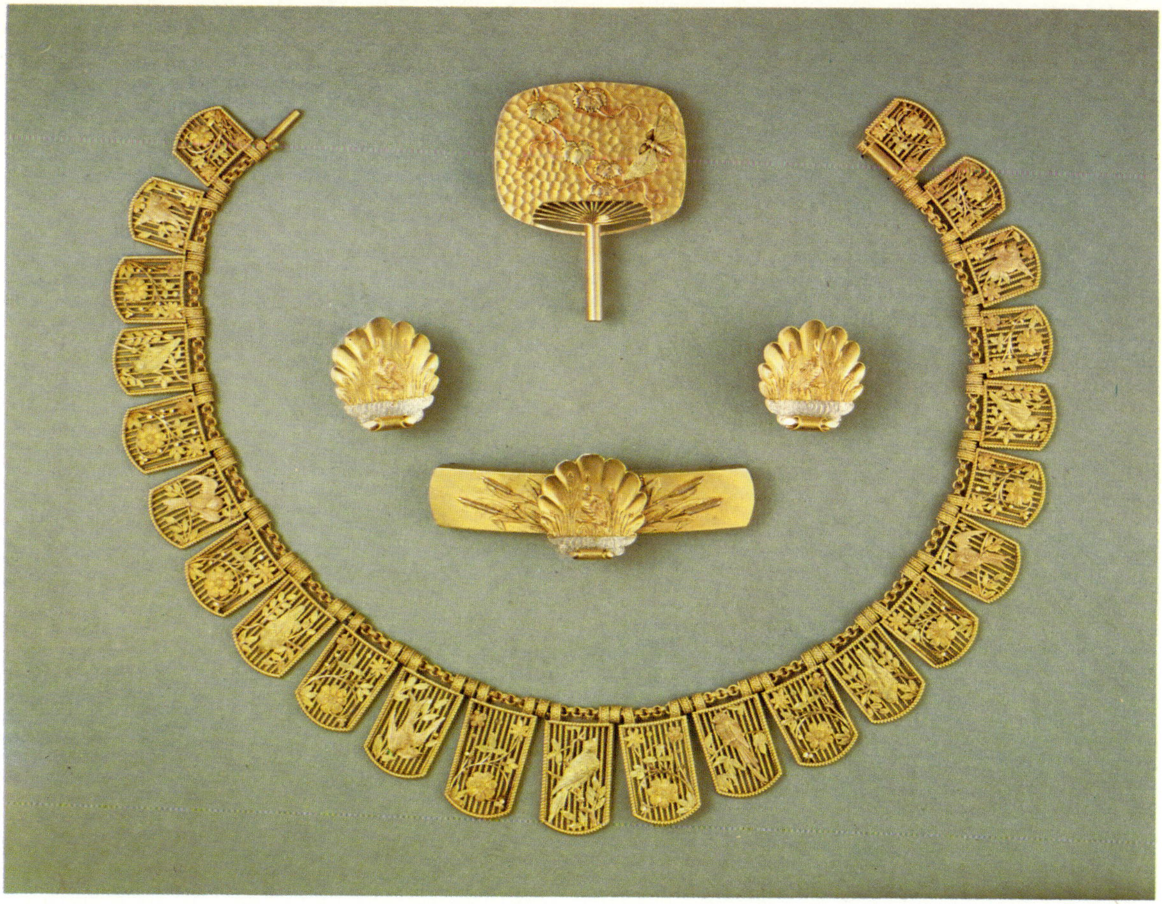

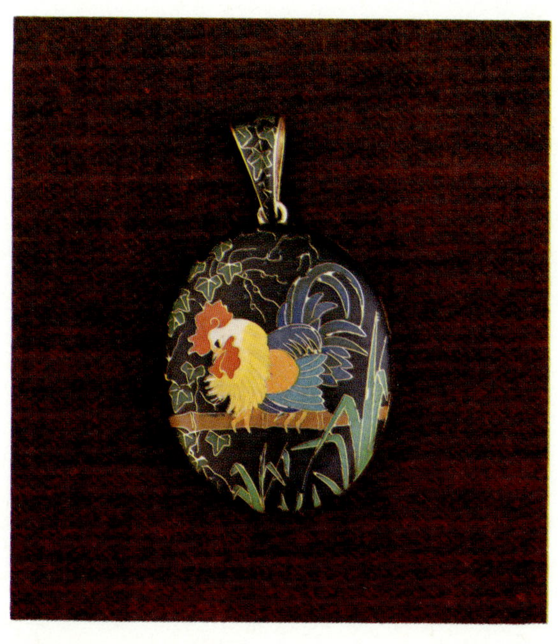

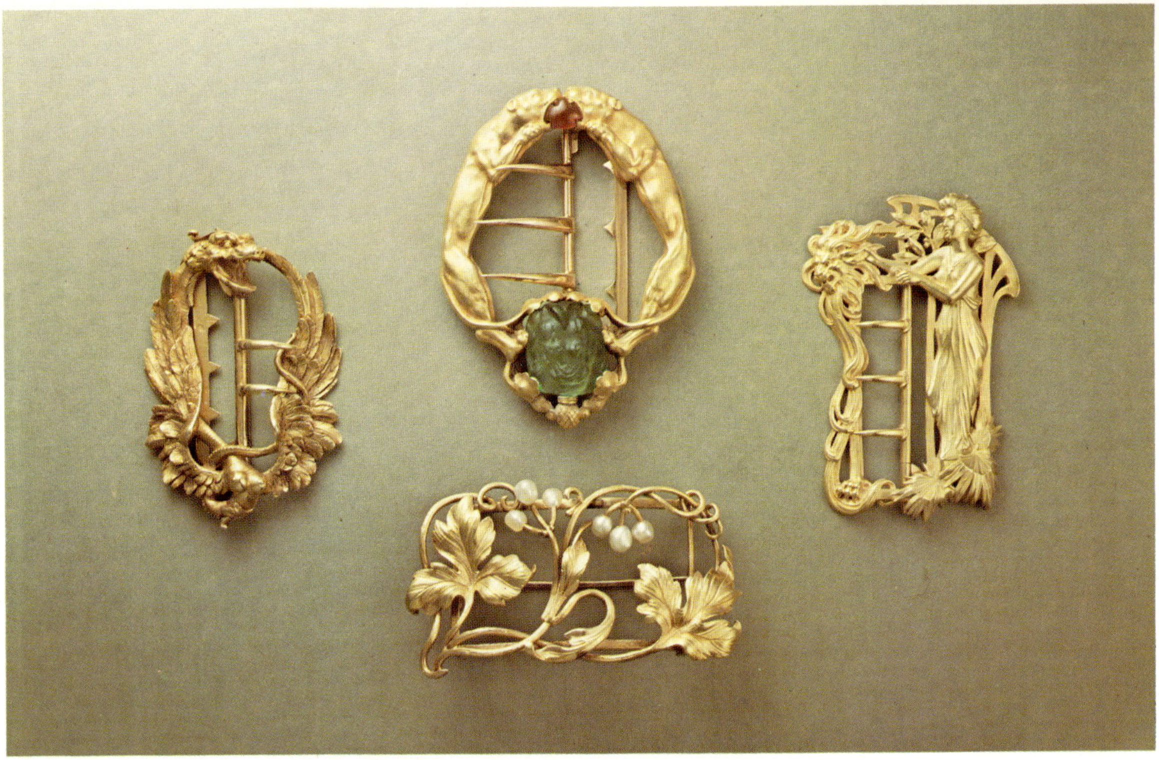

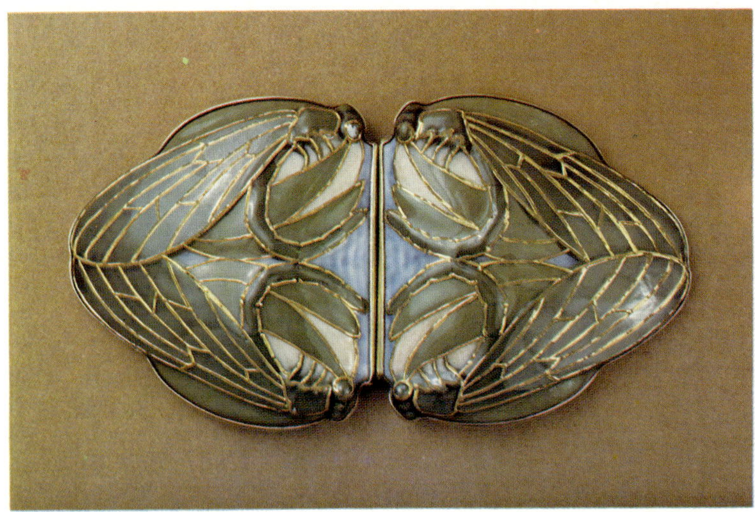

French Gold Art-Nouveau Jewellery, 1880–1905

Largest piece, double leopard buckle, H. 7·8 cm.

Copenhagen Porcelain Waist-clasp

After a design by Georg Jensen. Danish, *c.* 1902. W. 11·2 cm.

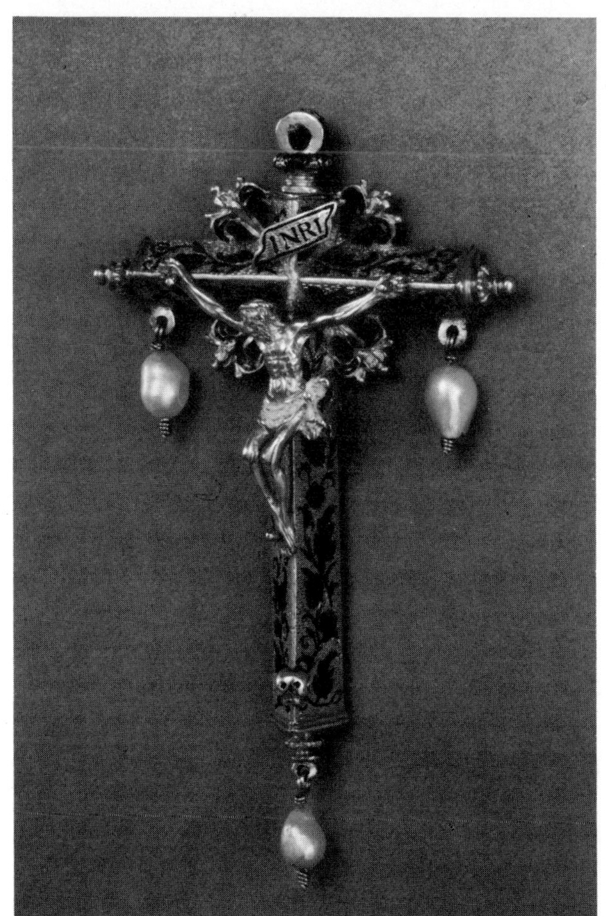 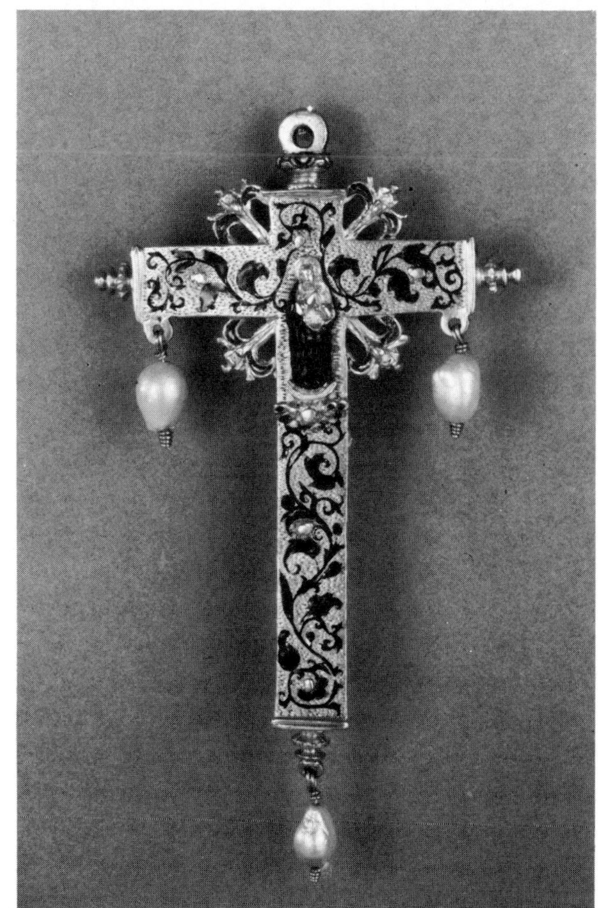

I

Enamelled gold pendant cross, with pendant pearls; on the reverse, enamelled gold applied relief depicting the Virgin Mary standing on the crescent moon, supported by a winged cherub. Spanish, first half of 17th century. H. (including pearl) 10·3 cm.

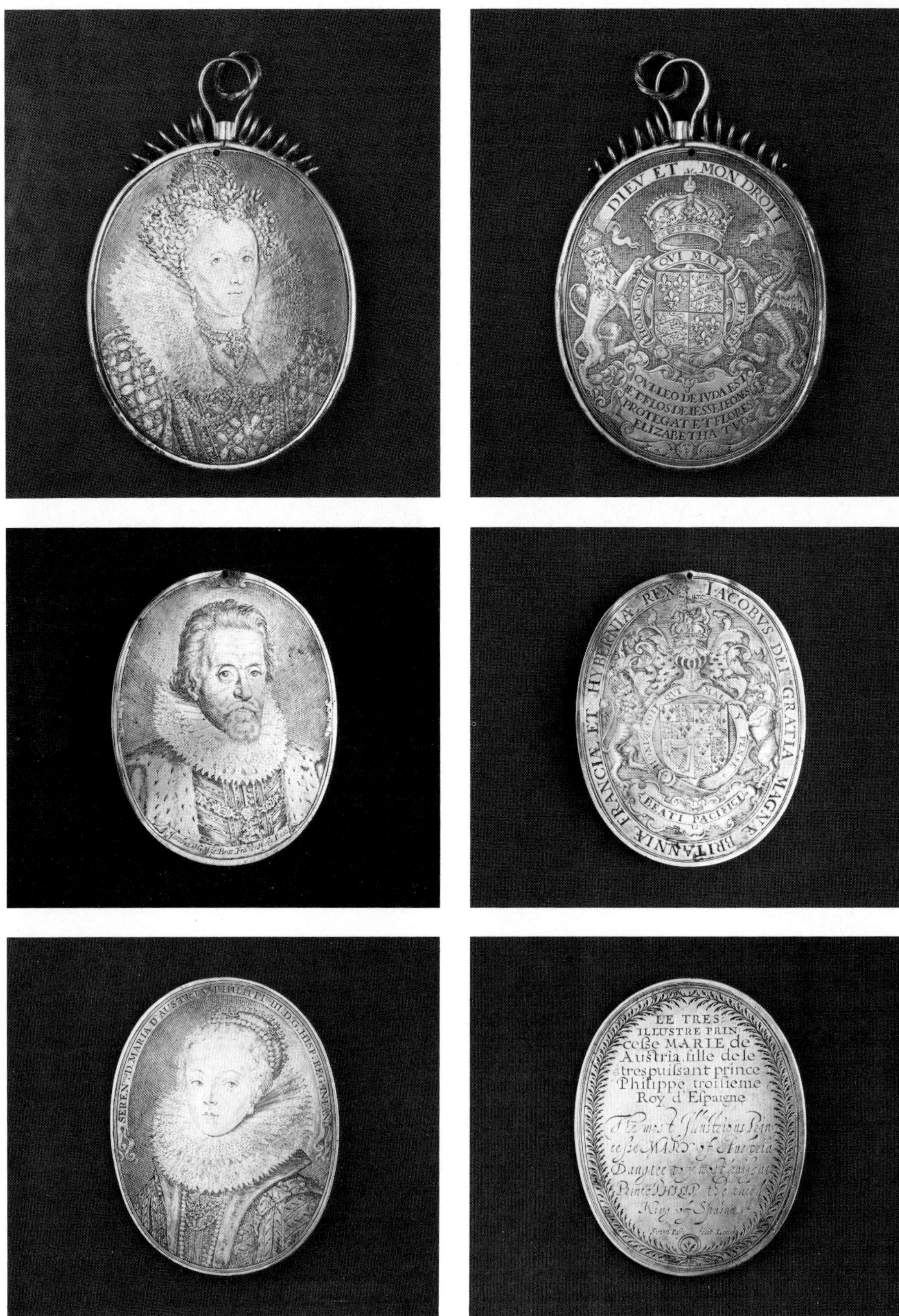

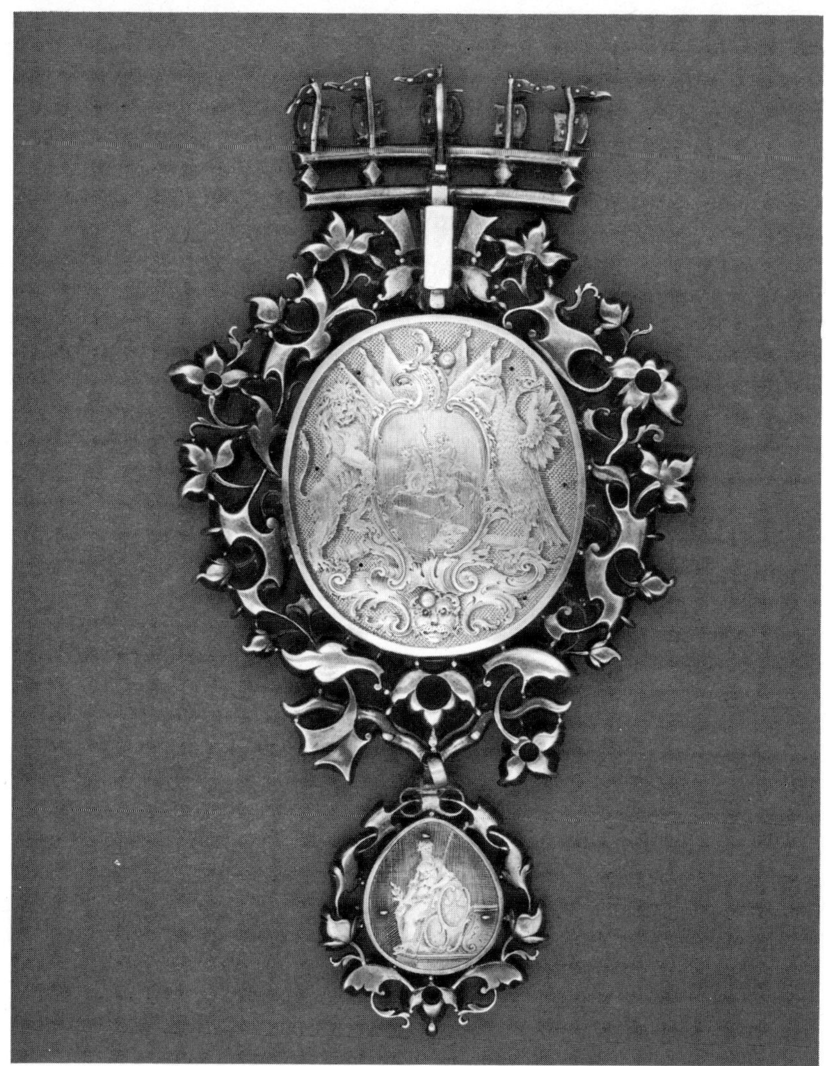

2

Three silver pendant medallions, engraved by Simon de Passe (1595–1647), working in London *c*. 1616–24.

Queen Elizabeth I of England; on the reverse, the Royal Arms, motto and inscription. L. 8 cm.

James I of England and VI of Scotland; on the reverse, the Royal Arms, motto and inscription. L. 5·8 cm.

Maria of Austria, daughter of Philip III of Spain; on the reverse, inscriptions in French and English and the signature in full *Simon Pass fecit Lond*. L. 5·6 cm.

3

Reverse of the Badge of the Anti-Gallican Society (see also Plate III); closed-back silver setting, with silver-gilt oval plaques engraved with the Society's heraldic device and, below, Britannia. English, mid-18th century. L. 14 cm.

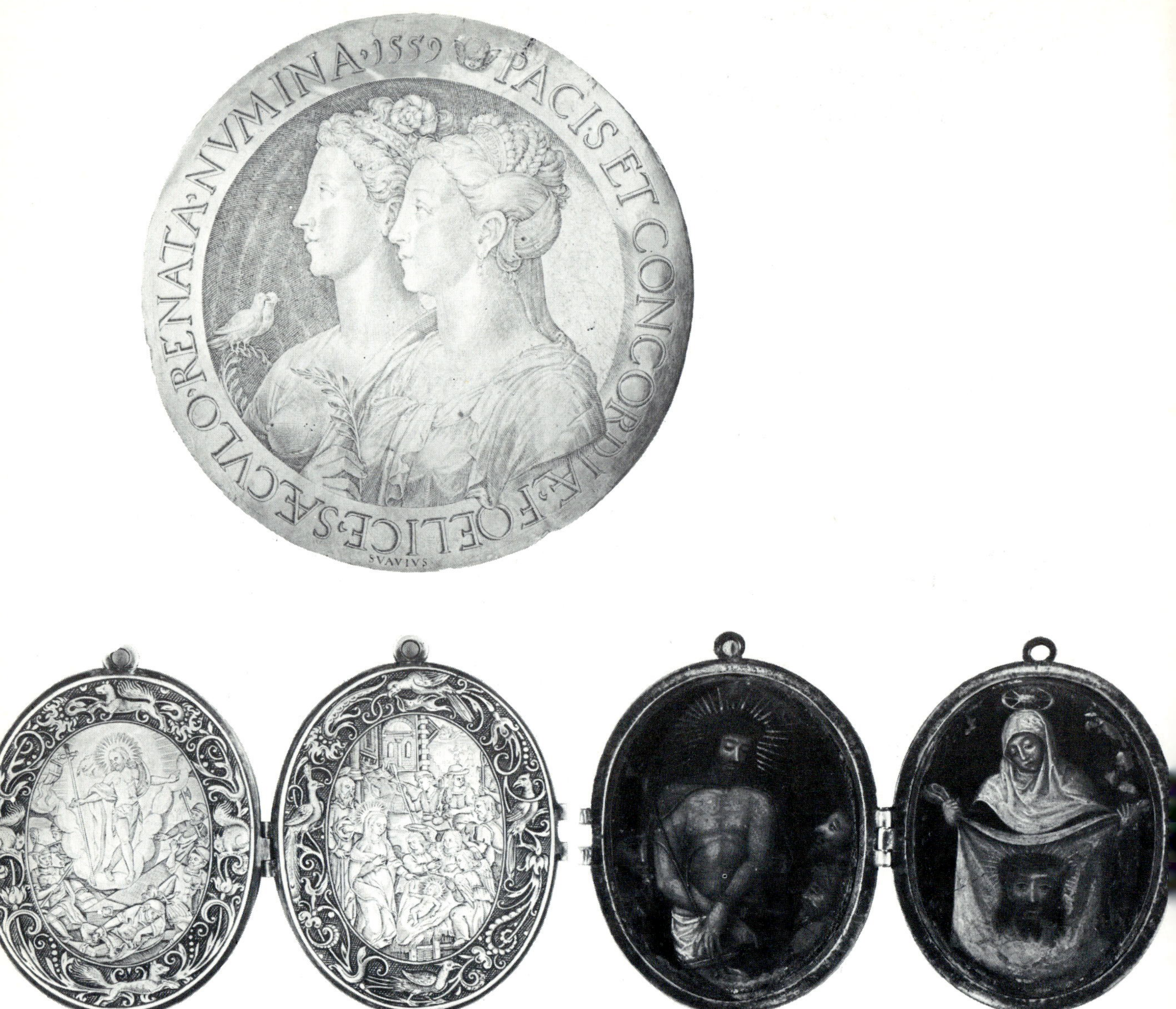

4

Silver roundel by Lambert Suavius, of Liège (about 1510–67); the inscription reads: PACIS ET CONCORDIÆ · FOELICE · SÆCVLO · RENATA · NVMINA · 1559. Probably made to commemorate the Peace of Cateau-Cambrésis between the Spanish and the French. D. 9·2 cm.

Engraved silver locket opening to reveal two painted miniatures of the 'Mocking of Christ' and 'St Veronica'. German, early 17th century. H. (including pendant loop) 5·7 cm.

5

Gold chain, composed of oblong, octagonal links inlaid with pitch (?), alternating with chased gold flower-heads. English, about 1600. L. 84·5 cm.

Silver spherical container, probably for a bezoar-stone, in two halves, the exterior decorated with silver-gilt pierced foliage laid over the hammered silver body. Perhaps English, 17th century. L. 7·5 cm.

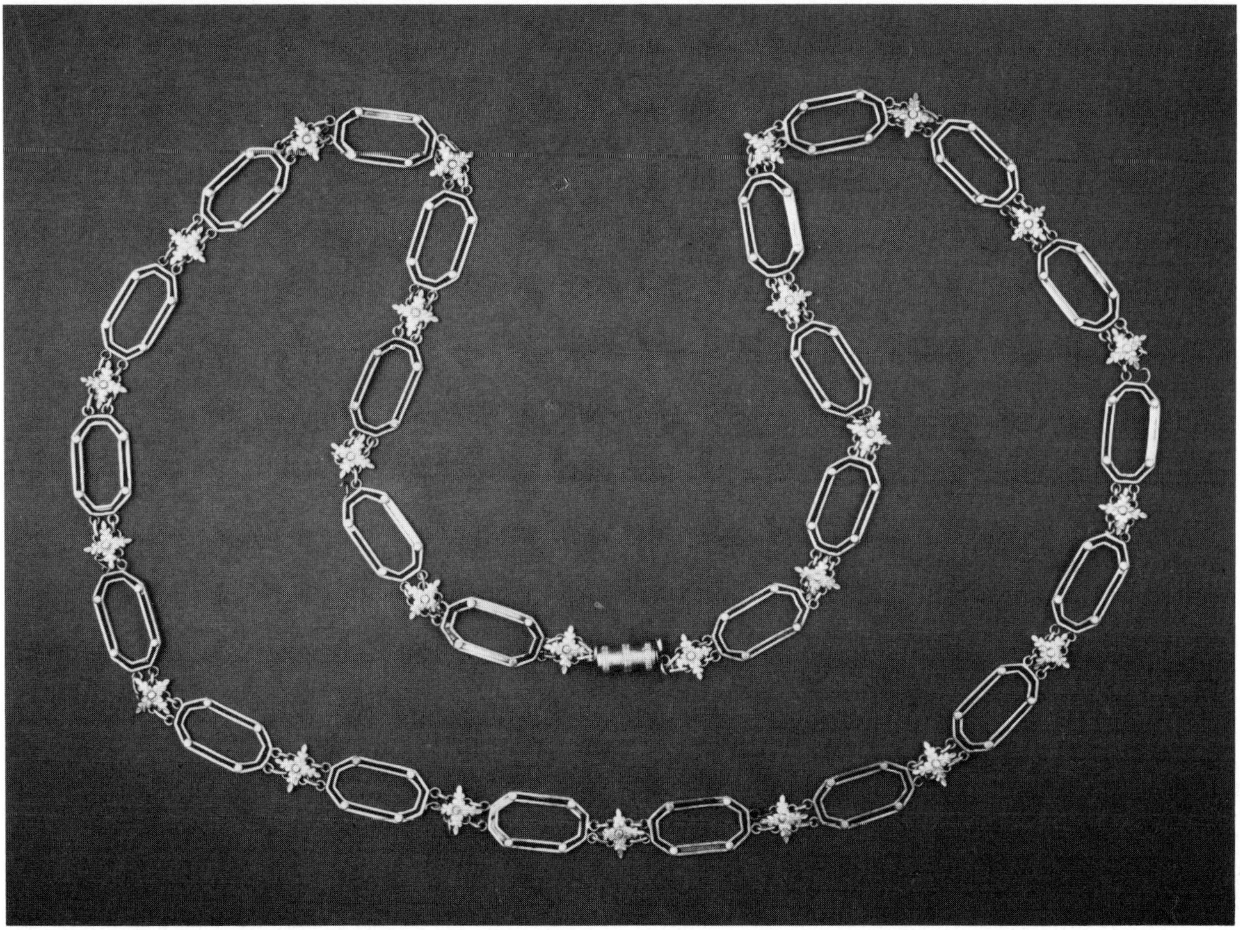

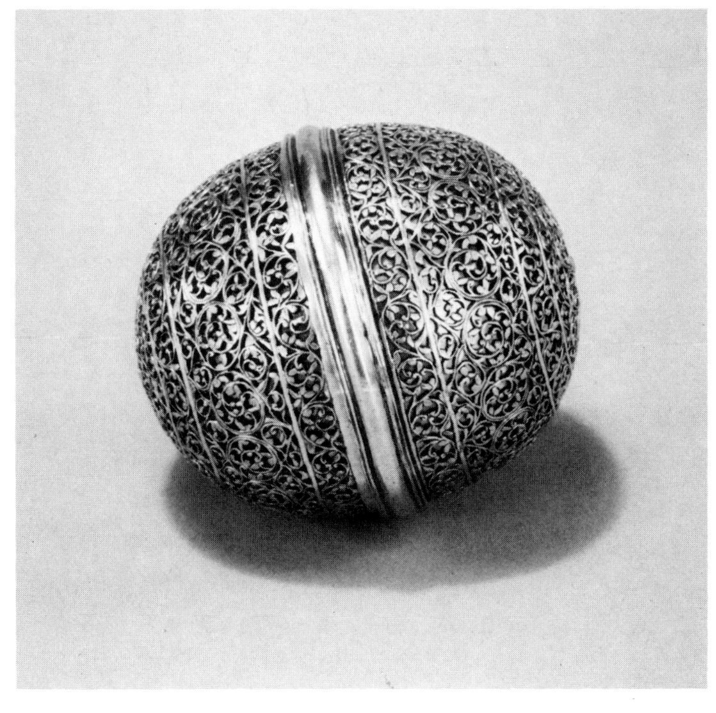

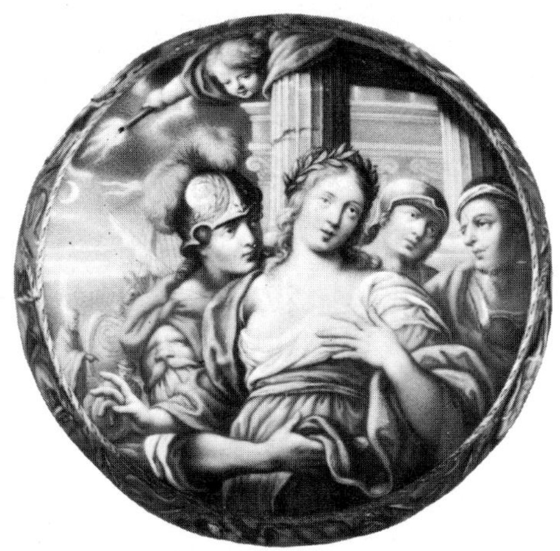
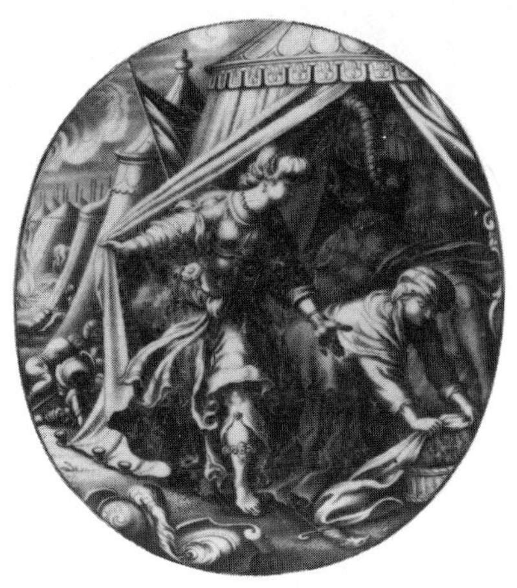

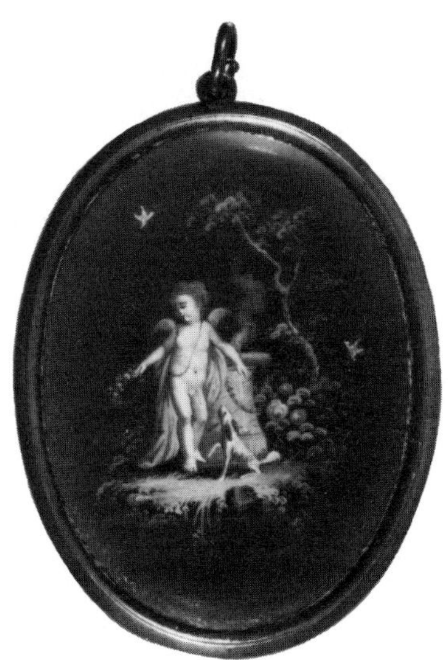

6

'The Rape of Helen', enamelled in Geneva, second half of 17th century. D. 5·1 cm.

'Judith in the Tent of Holophernes', enamelled in sepia monochrome. South German, second half of 17th century. H. 4·9 cm.

Oval purple glass pendant, painted with a miniature and flanked by two small birds in gold leaf, apparently overlaid with a layer of clear glass. French (?), early 18th century. H. (including pendant loop) 5·8 cm.

7

Necklace of painted enamel plaques, monochrome landscapes interspersed with single figures; on the reverse, stylised flowers and leaves in colour. Details of the landscape links and of floral enamelling on the reverse. Probably Dutch, about 1650. L. 41 cm.

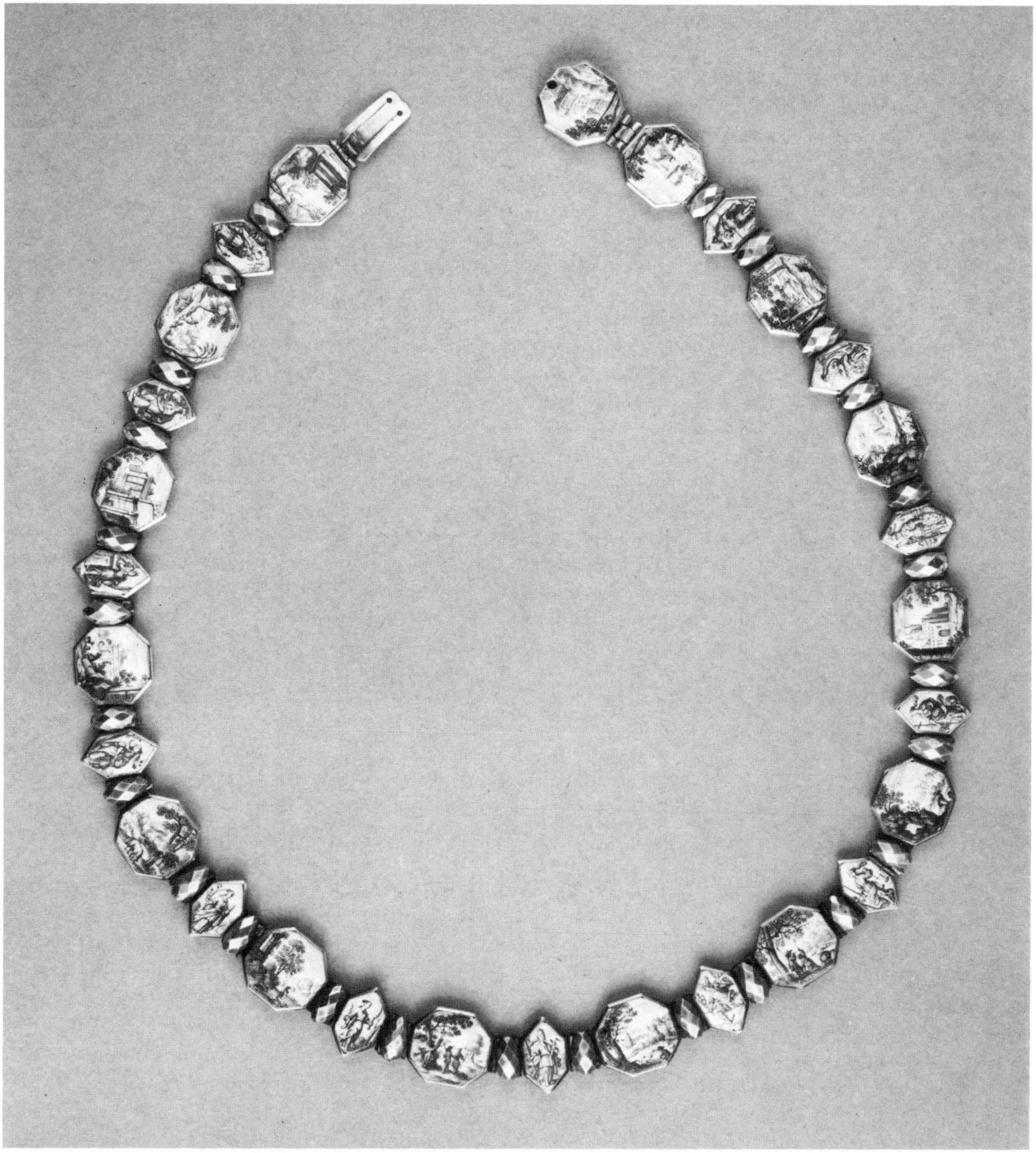

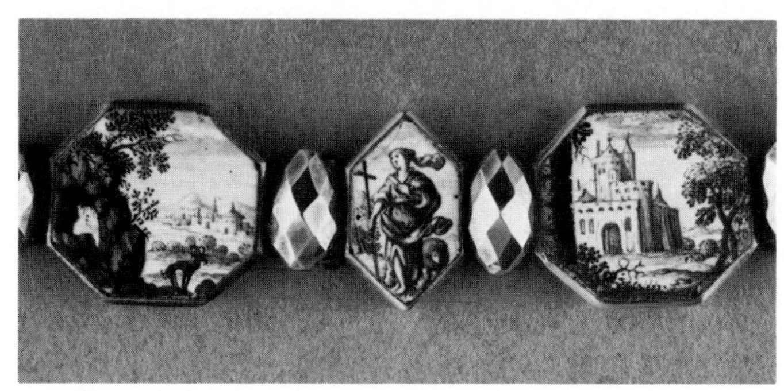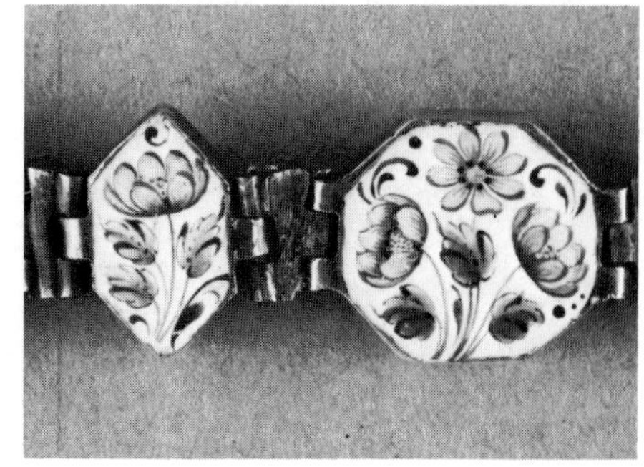

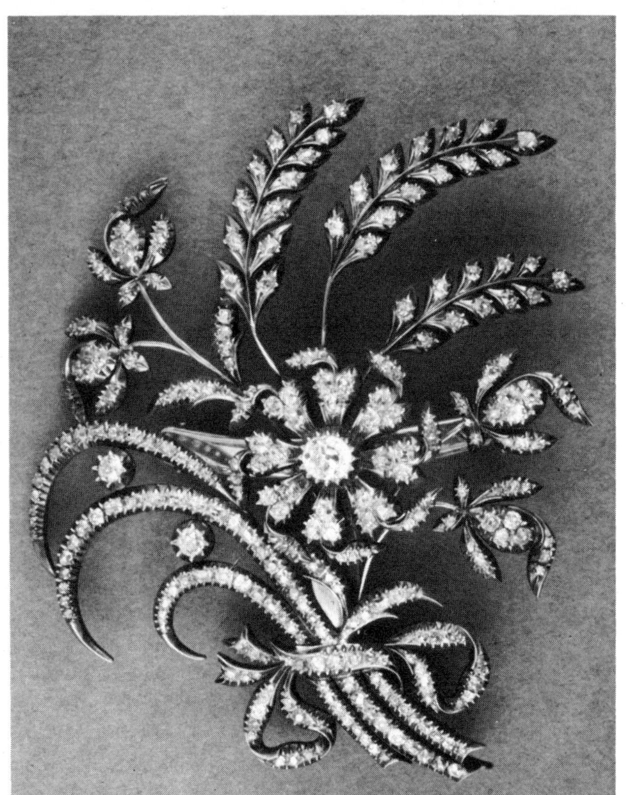

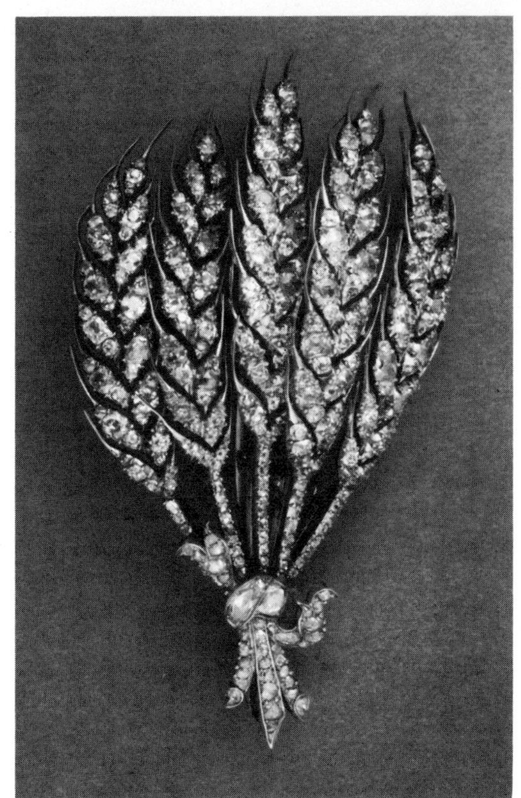

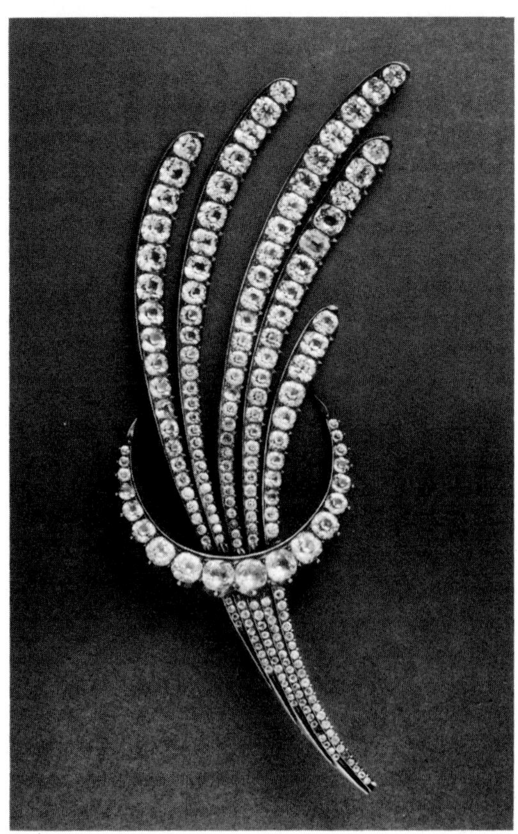

8

French and English 18th-century gem-set Aigrettes

Spray of flowers and wheat-ears, set *à-jour* in silver and gold. L. 9·2 cm.

Bunch of wheat-ears, set *à-jour* in silver and gold. L. 10·1 cm.

Crescent and spray aigrette, pastes in a closed-back silver setting. L. 13·4 cm.

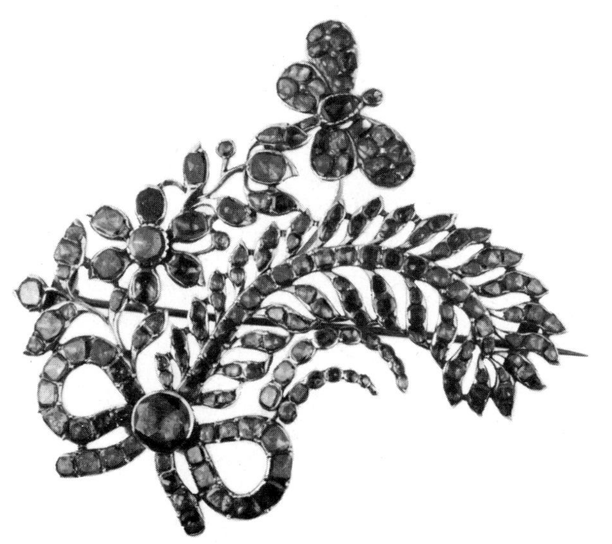

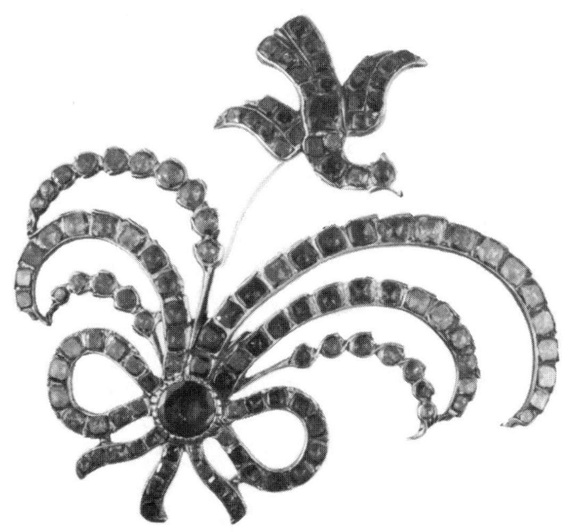

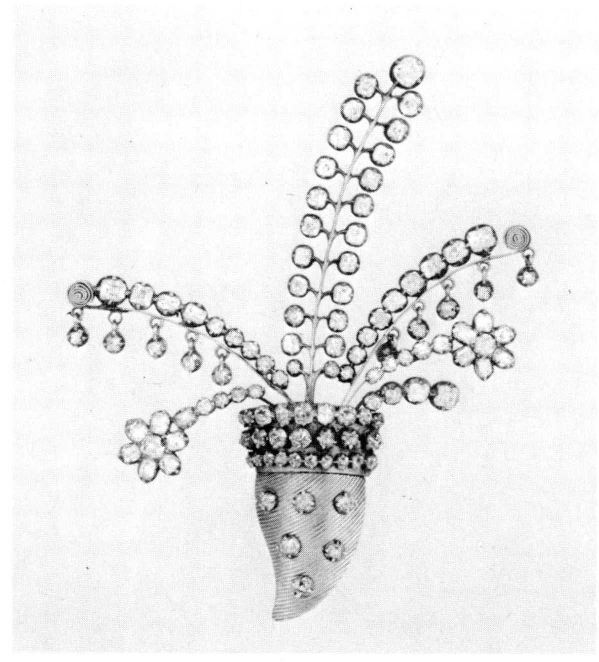

9

18th-century gem-set Aigrettes

Butterfly on a spray; gold set with garnets. English, about 1760. W. 7·1 cm.

Bird on a spray; gold set with garnets. English, about 1760. W. 6·6 cm.

Silver and gold cornucopia with gem-set flower-spray, ornamented with gold cannetille-work. Italian (Sicilian?), late 18th century. L. 6·9 cm.

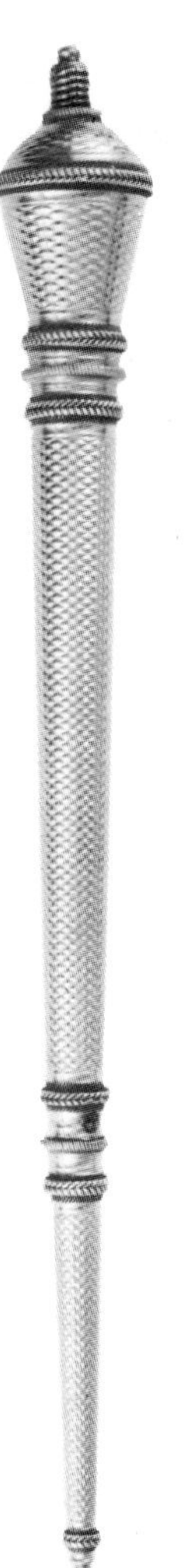

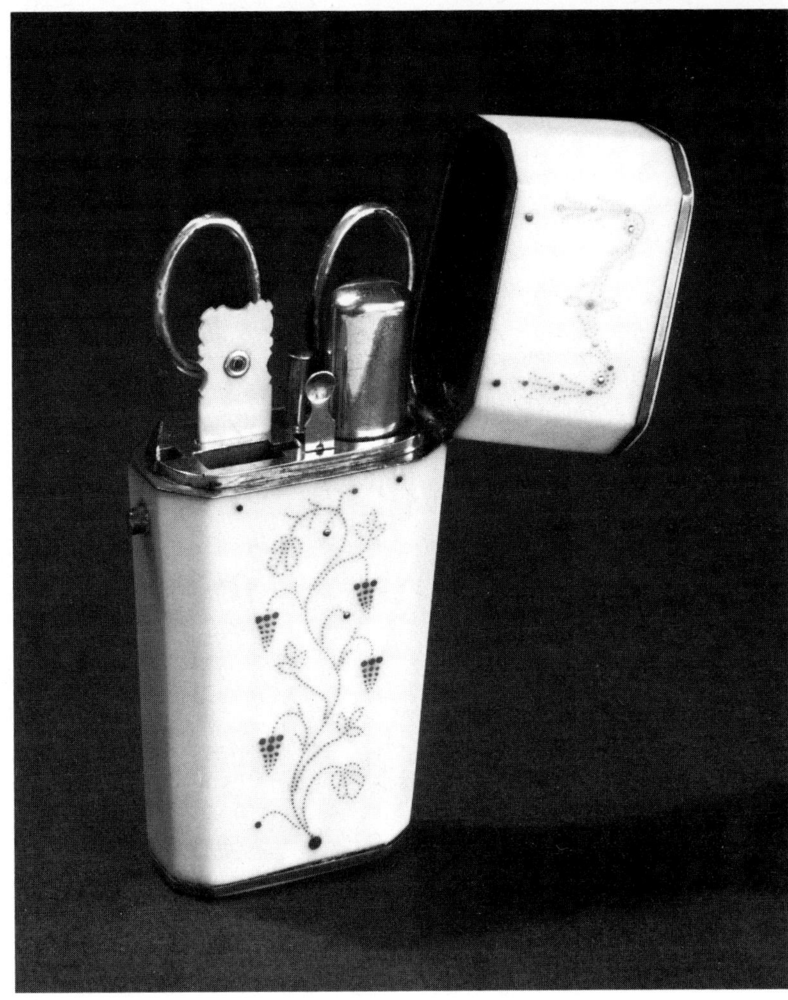

10

Tambour-hook holder, engine-turned, three-coloured gold. French, about 1760. L. 13·1 cm.

Ivory *necessaire*, ornamented with *piqué-point*. French, mid-18th century. W. (at opening) 4 cm.

11

Gold-mounted mother-of-pearl box with ciselé decoration, English, about 1730–40. W. 7 cm.

Ivory box, with inscription MA CARGAISON SONT DES BOMBONS. English, about 1780. D. 7·3 cm.

Gold and tortoiseshell presentation box, given by George IV to his chef, John Watier, the founder of Watier's Club, dated 1815. W. 8·6 cm.

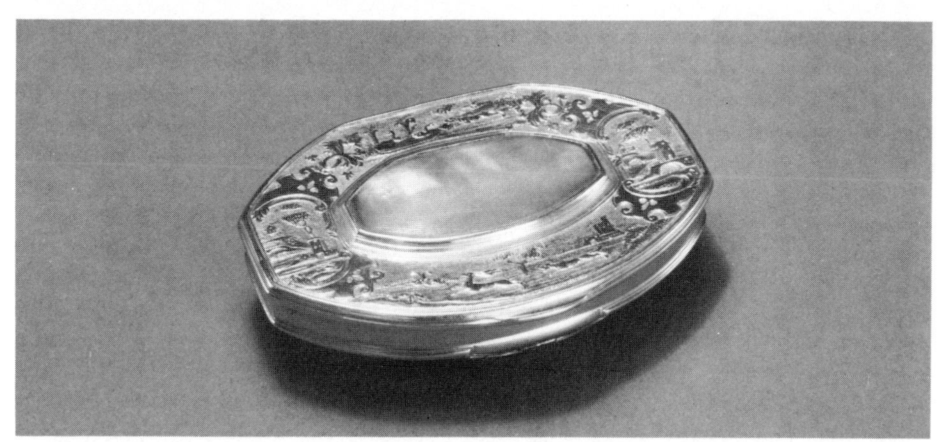

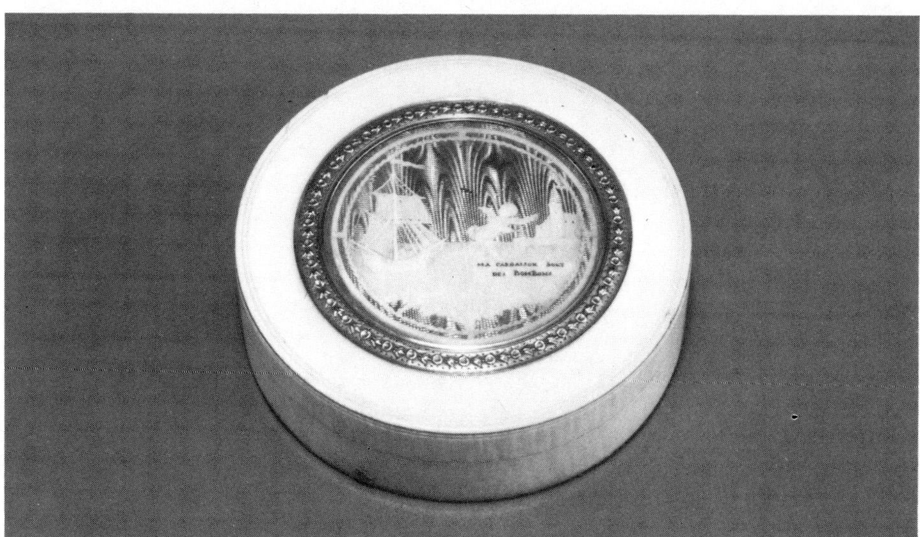

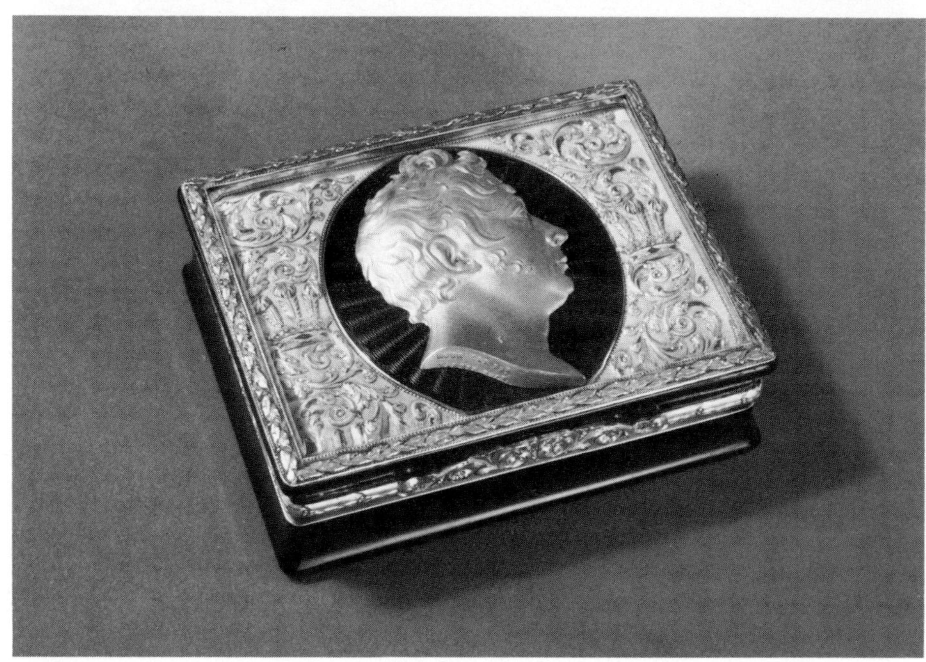

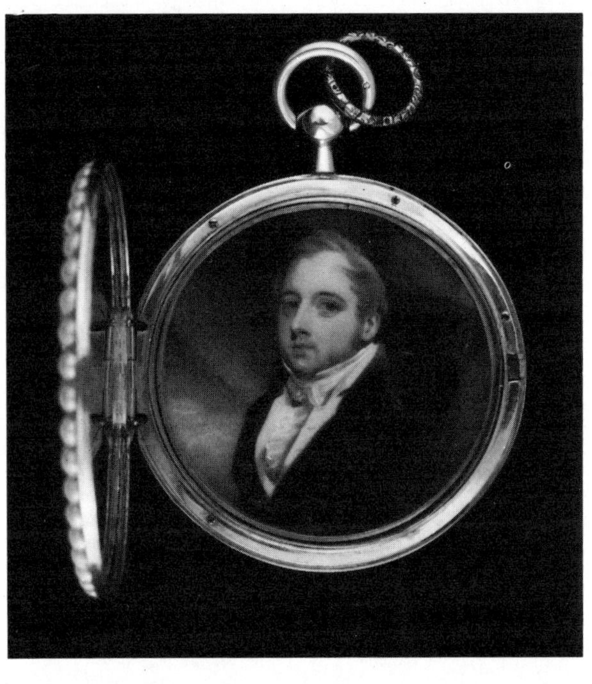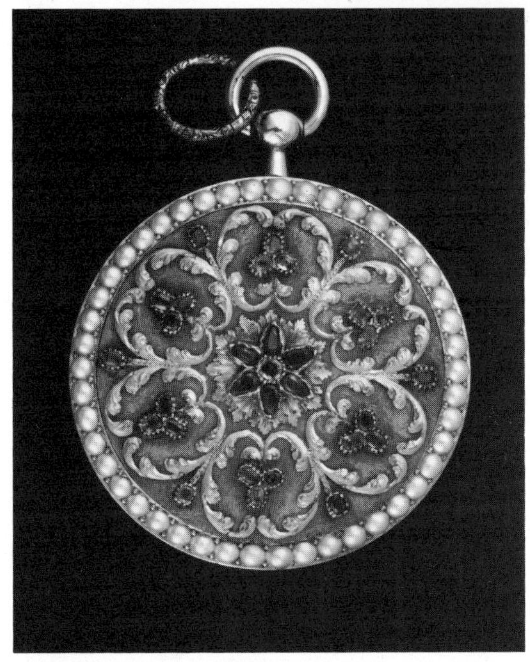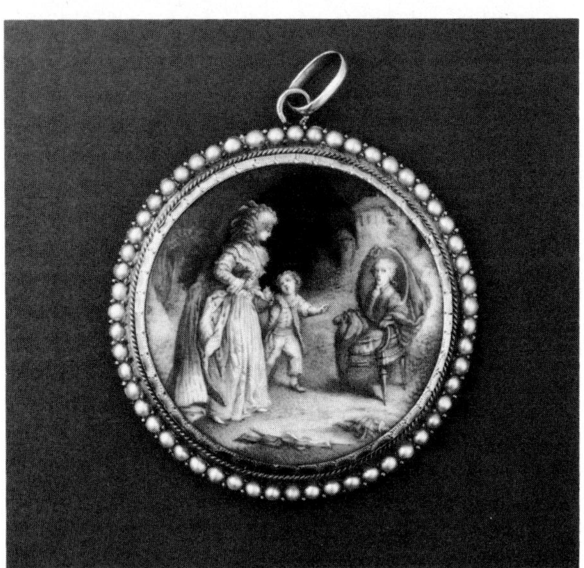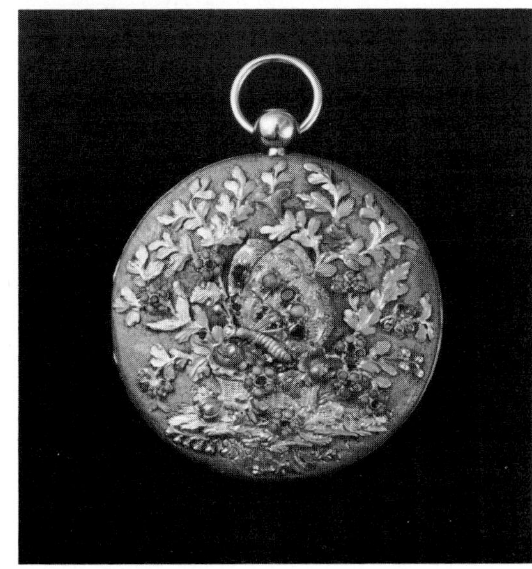

12

Gold miniature case: open, showing a painted portrait of a man; shut, showing the coloured gold garnet-set ornament and border of pearls. English, about 1830. D. 5·2 cm.

Mourning miniature painted in *grisaille* touched with blue, the gold setting bordered with pearls. English or French, 1770–80. D. 5·1 cm.

Gold miniature case, coloured gold and gem-set ornament, opening to reveal a miniature compartment. English about, 1830. D. 4·3 cm.

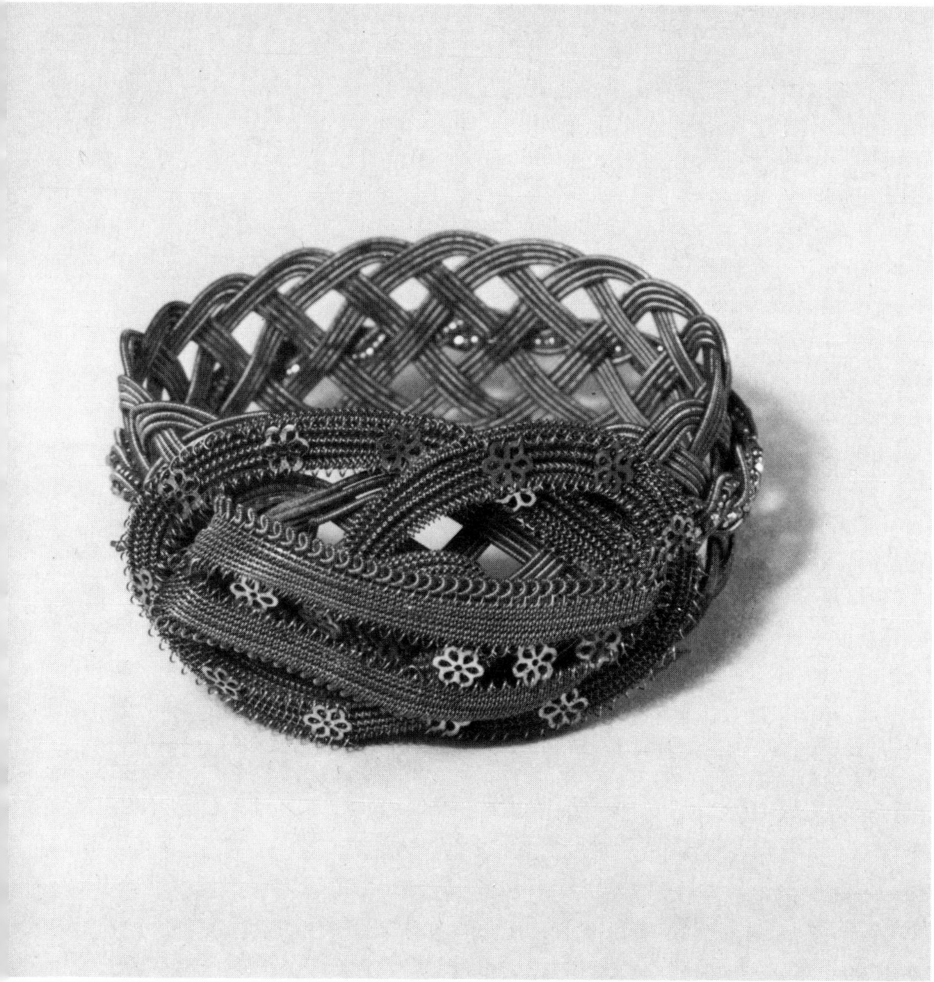

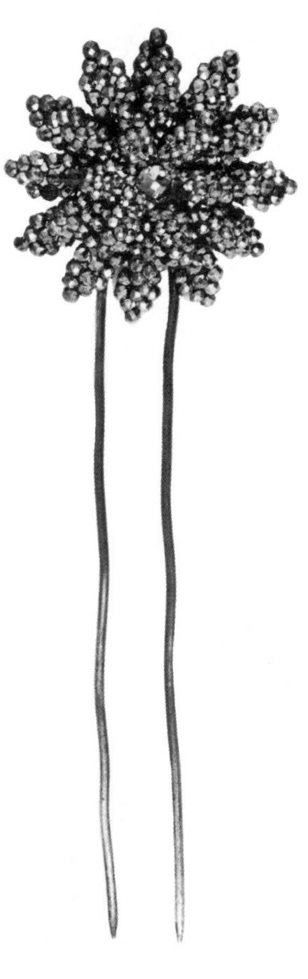

13

Fine interlaced steel-work mesh bracelet, ornamented with polished cut-steel pailettes. English, about 1800. D. 6·2 cm.

Hair-pin ornament in the form of a double flower-head in facet-cut steel studs. English, about 1800. D. 3·6 cm.

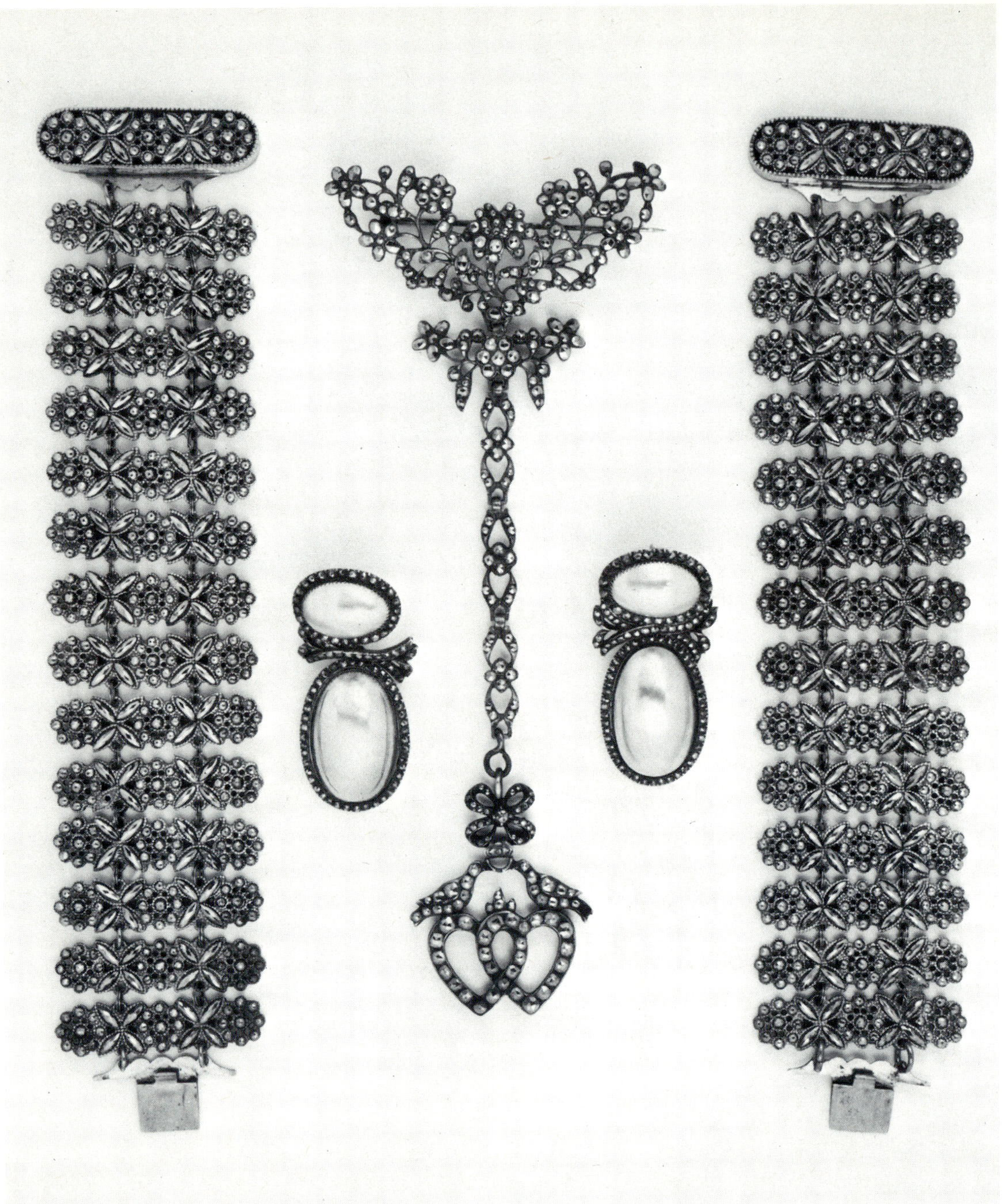

14

Group of cut-steel and iron pyrite (marcasite) jewellery, pair of bracelets of facet-cut steel, earrings with 'pearl' centres, pendant of iron pyrites. English, 1790–1800. L. (bracelets) 18·9 cm.

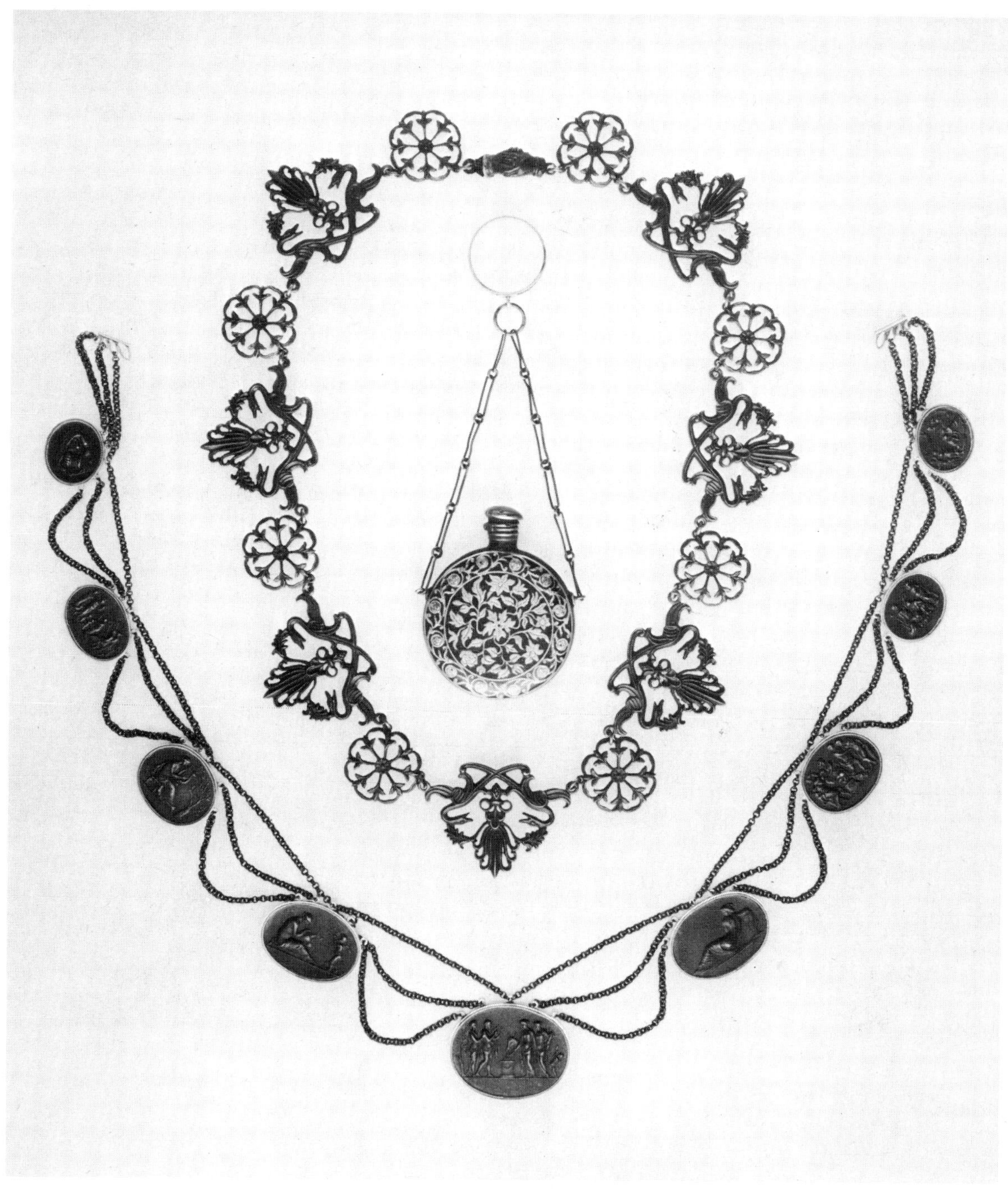

15

Group of 'Berlin' iron and gold jewellery, two necklaces and a finger-ring with pendant scent bottle. German, early 19th century. L. (scent bottle) 5·1 cm.

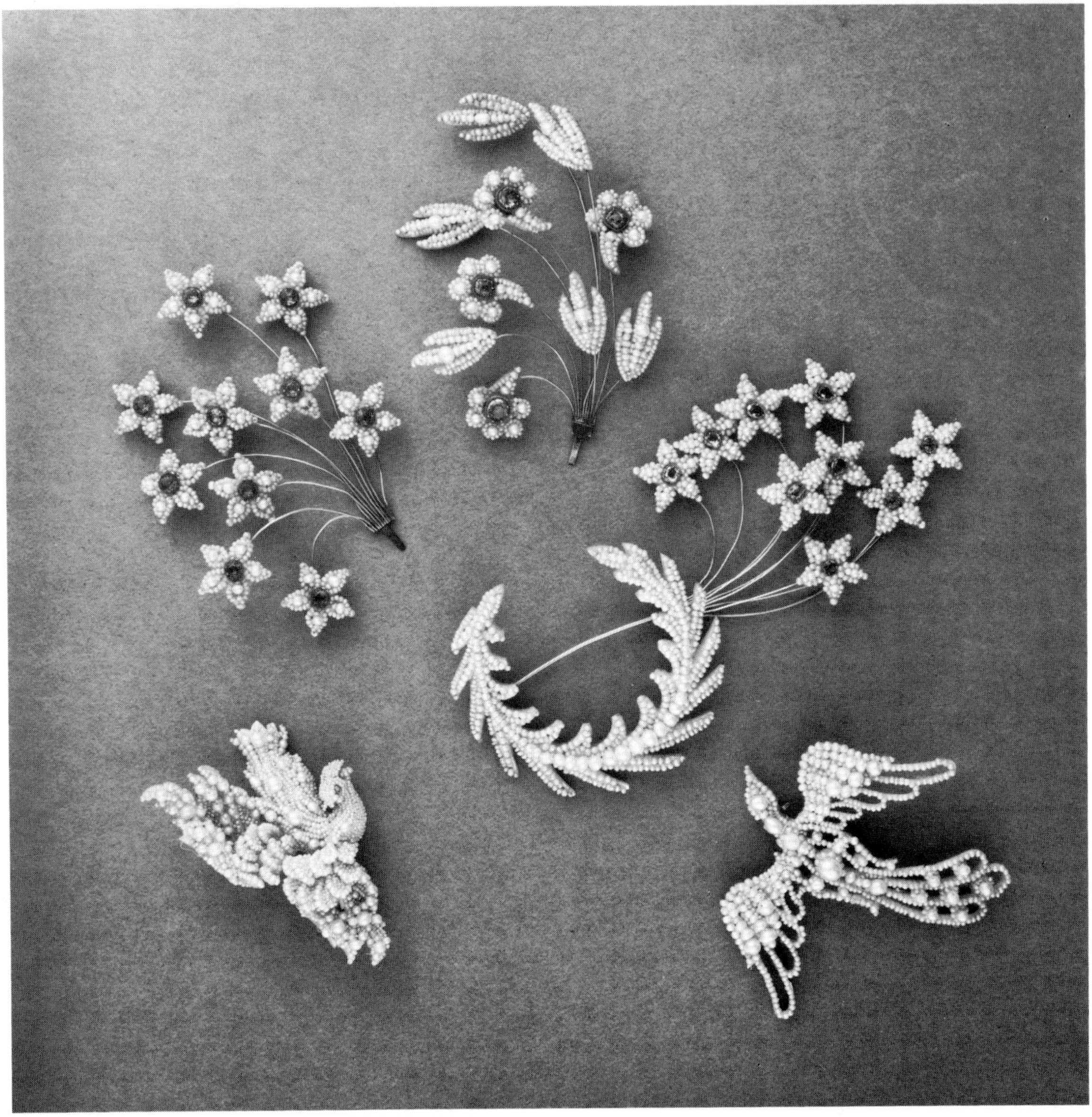

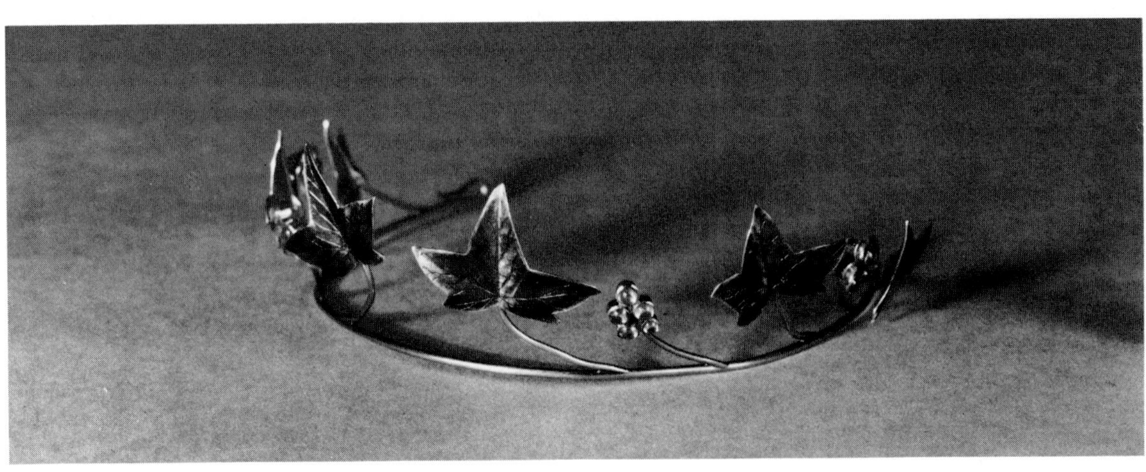

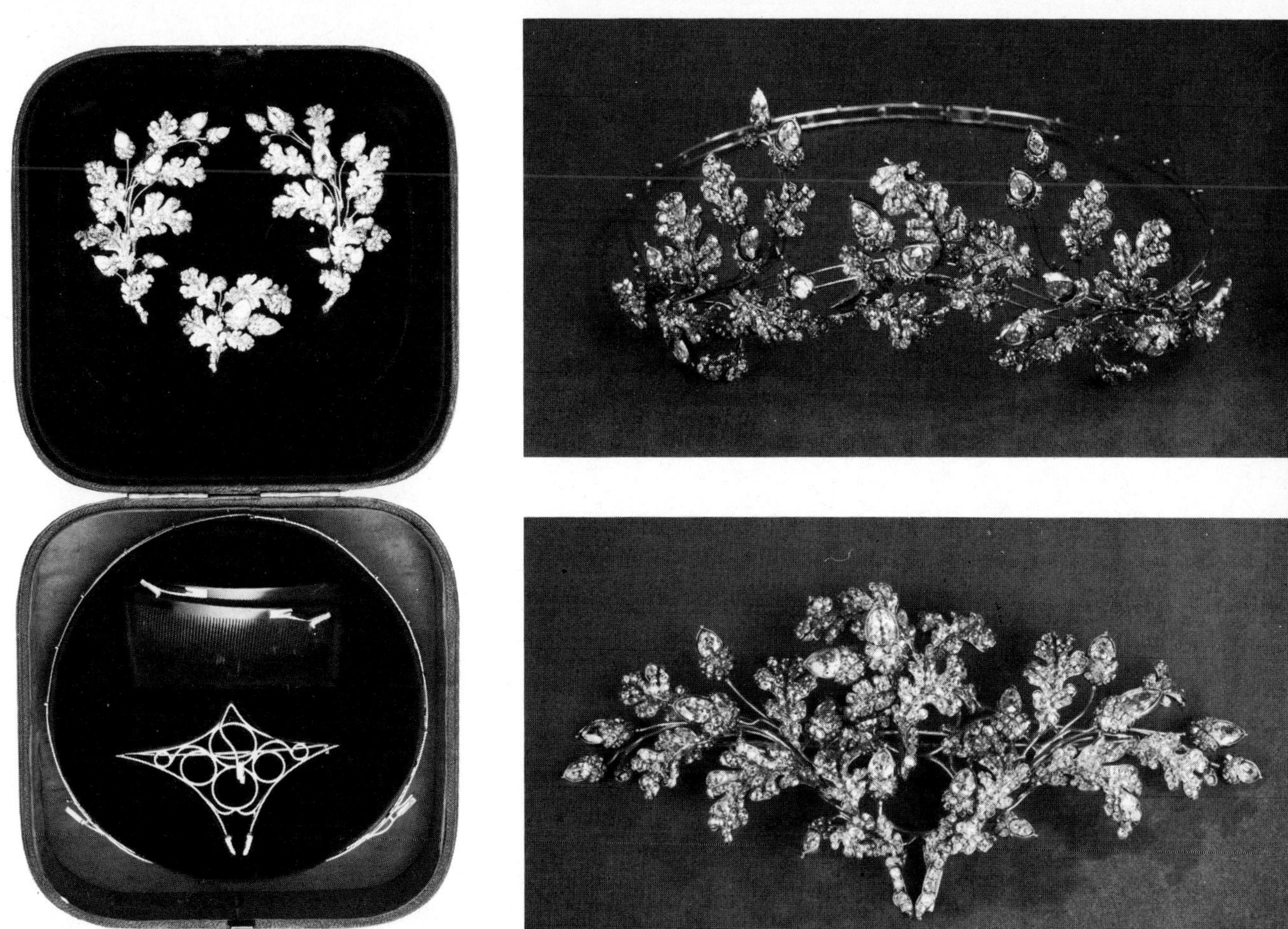

16

Set of interchangeable seed-pearl hair ornaments with different coloured stones in each spray; birds, flowers and a crescent. English, 1820–30. L. (flower spray) 8·5 cm.

Tiara, enamelled gold ivy-leaves alternating with fruits set with clusters of chrysophrases. By Carlo and Arthur Giuliano of London, after 1896. L. (of central leaf) 4·8 cm. D. 12·7 cm.

17

Case fitted for a set of diamond jewellery, showing the fittings for combs, tiara and brooch, the lid stamped with a Viscount's coronet and the initials 'M.P.'. English, 1840–50.

Diamond tiara assembled from the three brooches in the case on the gold wirework frame. W. 11·2 cm.

The same brooches reassembled to form a large corsage ornament. W. 16·3 cm.

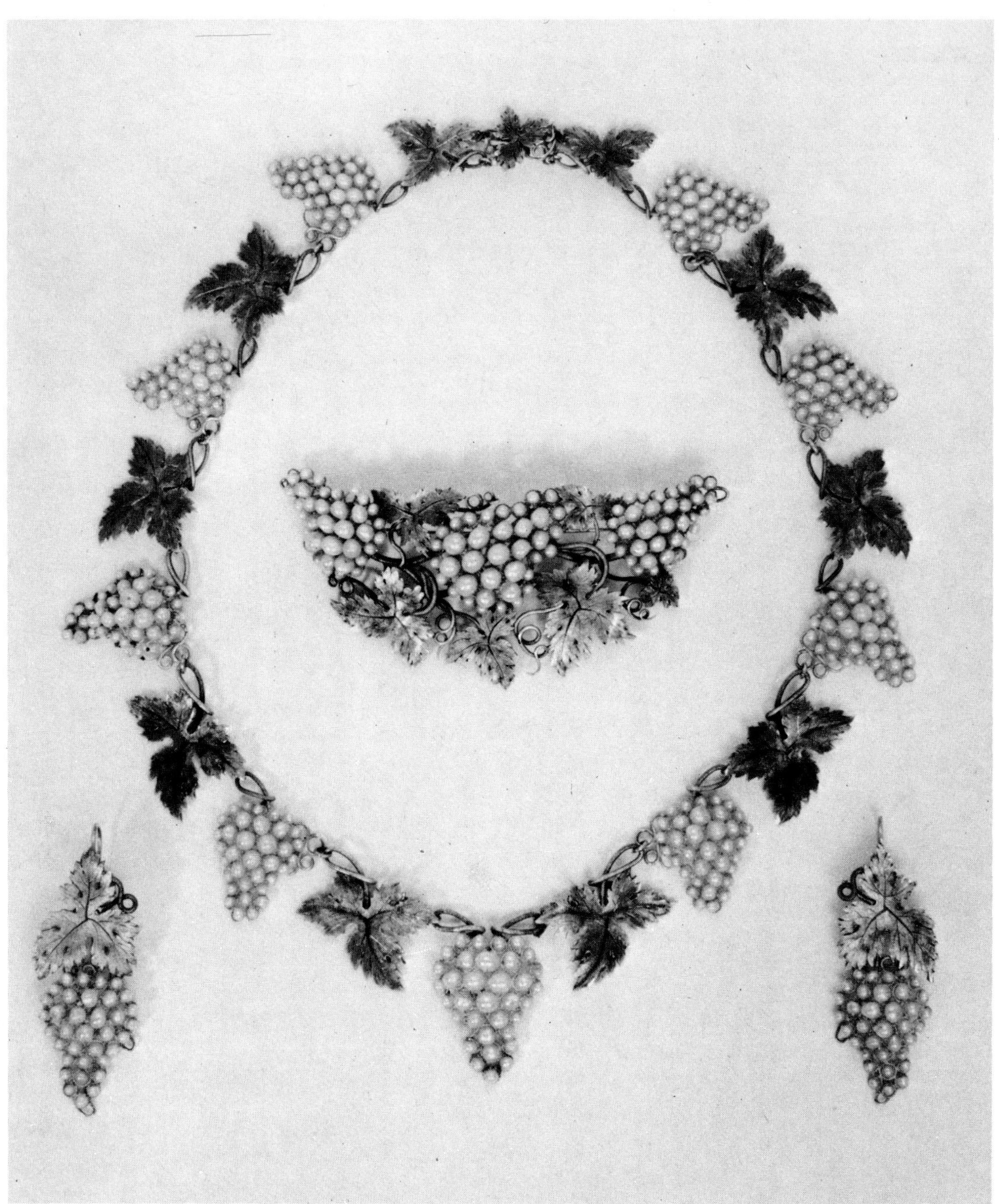

18

Parure: necklace, brooch and earrings, fruiting vine in bloomed and chased gold and seed-pearls. English, about 1830. W. (brooch) 7·6 cm.

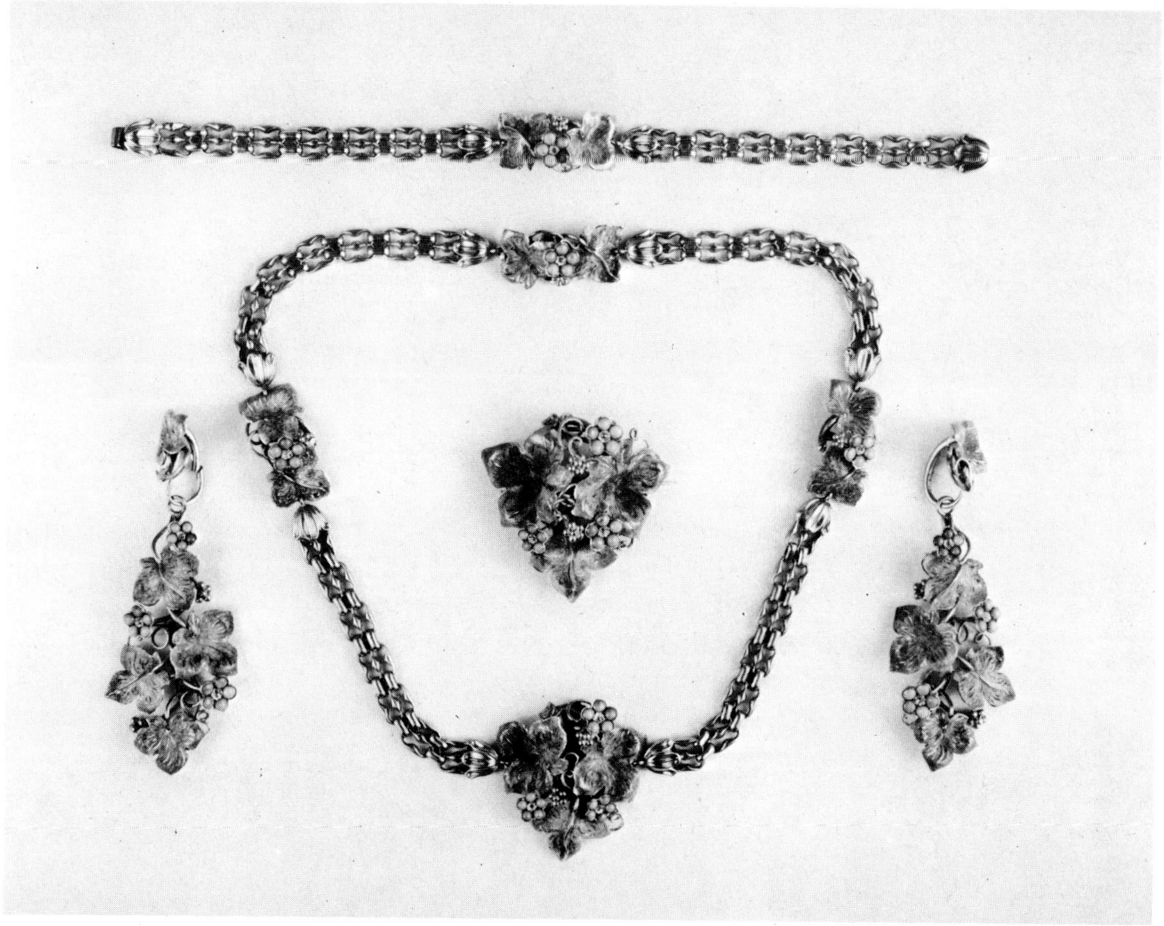

19

Parure: necklace, bracelet, brooch and earrings, bloomed and chased three-colour gold set with turquoises. Made by Mortimer & Hunt, London, about 1840 (the firm traded in this name from 1839–46). L. (brooch) 3·7 cm.

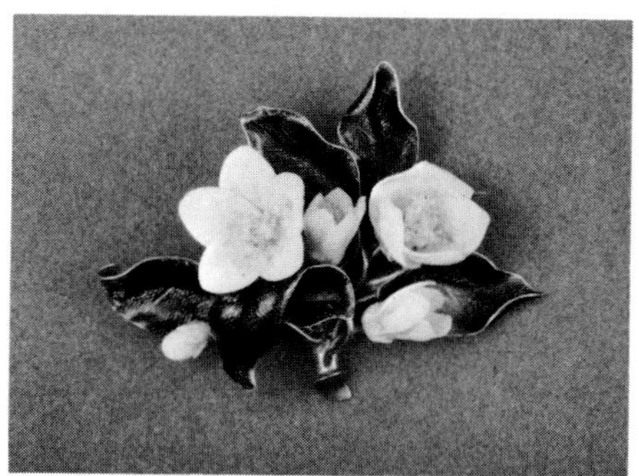 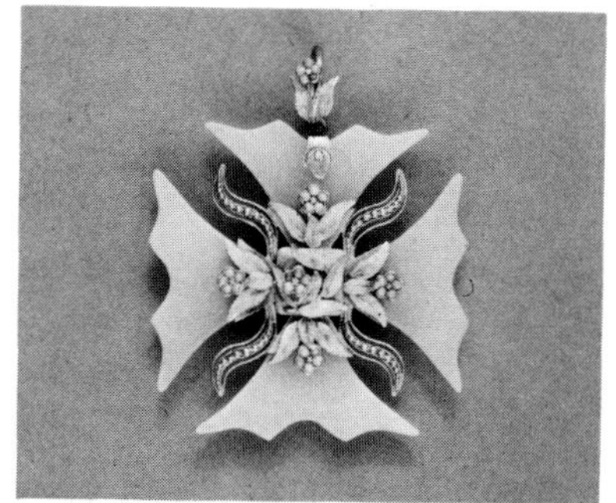

Brooch, in the form of a spray of orange blossom, enamelled gold with porcelain flower-heads, made by Hunt & Roskell, about 1846. This piece is related to a set of jewellery given by Prince Albert to Queen Victoria in 1845. The firm of Mortimer & Hunt became Hunt & Roskell in 1846. W. 6·8 cm.

Maltese cross pendant, chalcedony in a setting of coloured gold set with turquoises; in the reverse, a vinaigrette case with a hinged lid. English, about 1830. L. 6·4 cm.

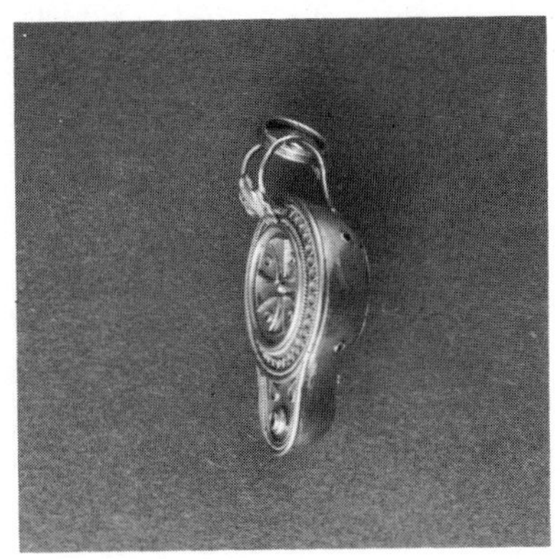 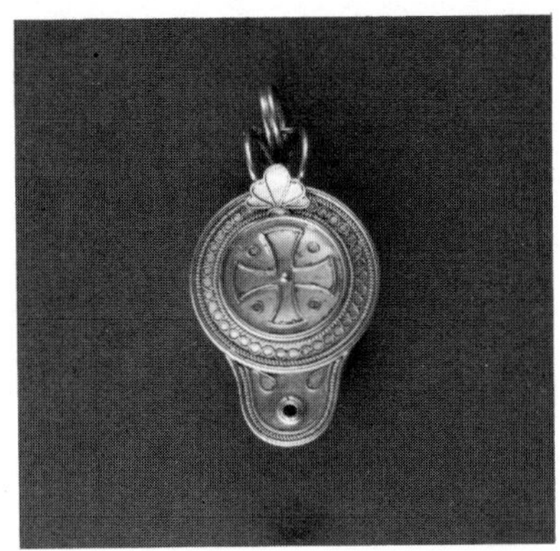 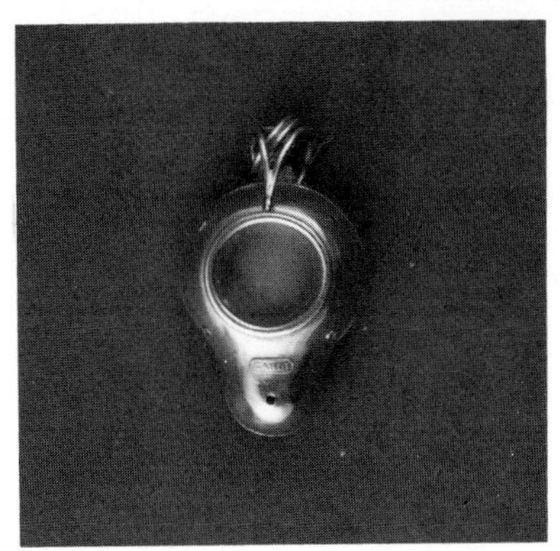

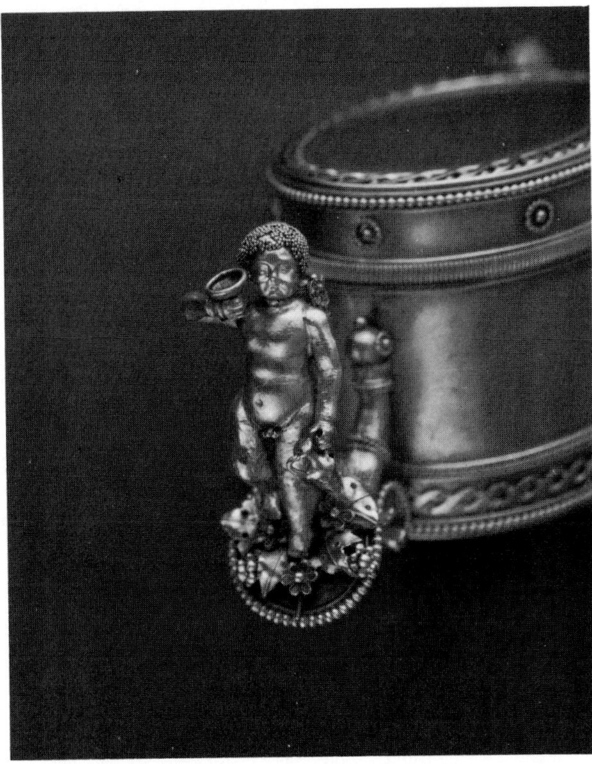

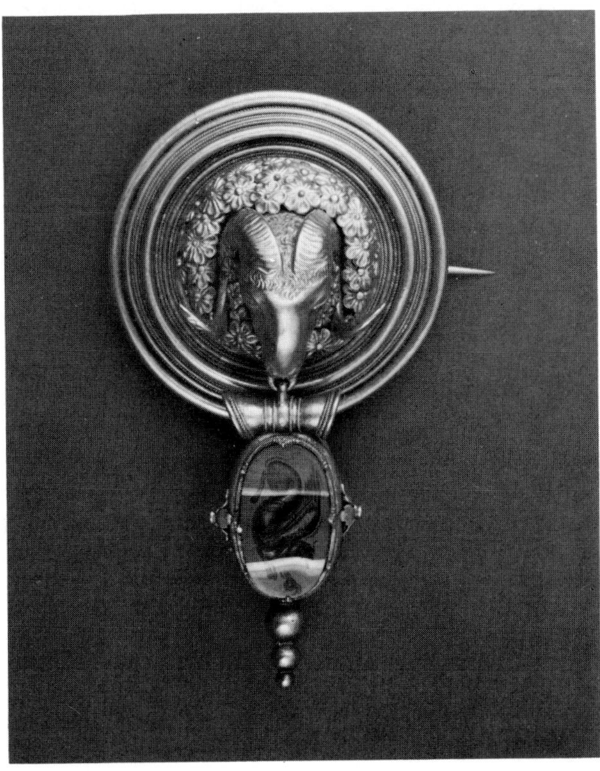

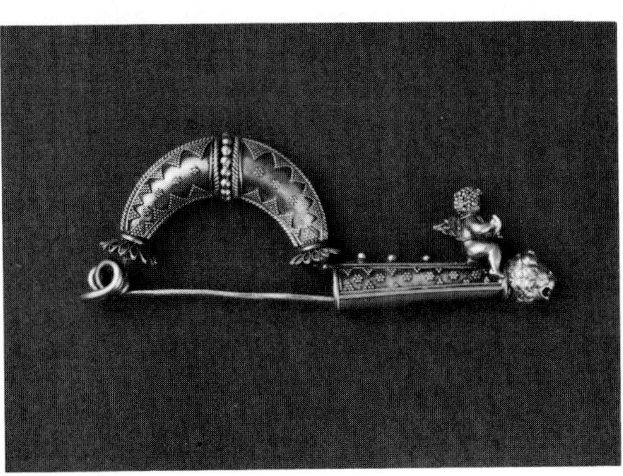

20

Three views of a gold pendant in the form of a Roman lamp, marked 'CARLI'. Rome, about 1860. L. 3·5 cm.

Detail of a box-handle, gold ornamented with field and pattern grain work. Probably by Giacinto Melillo. Naples, about 1880. W. (complete box) 7 cm.

Brooch, horned ram's head encircled by flowers in gold, agate intaglio pendant. By Ernesto Pierret. Rome, about 1870. L. 8·6 cm.

Bow-fibula brooch. Probably from the Melillo workshop, Naples, about 1880. W. 5·9 cm.

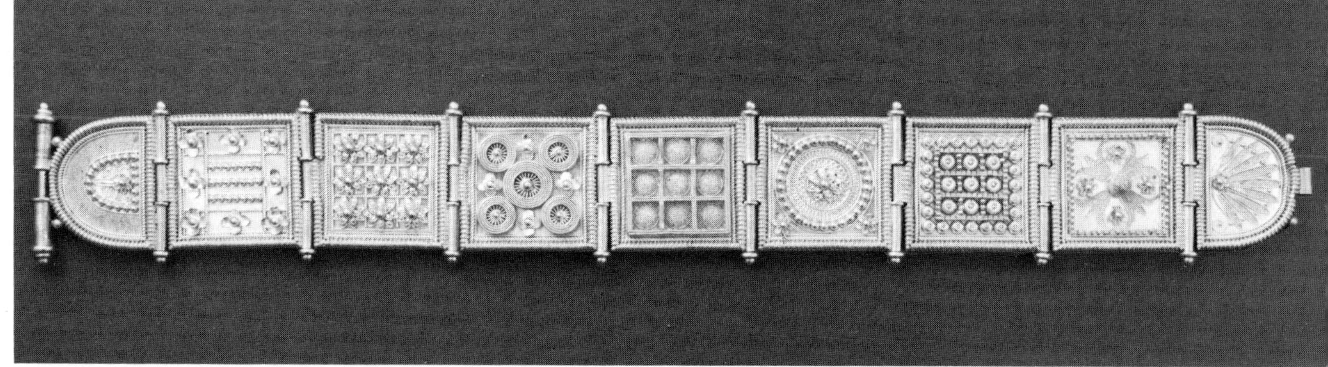

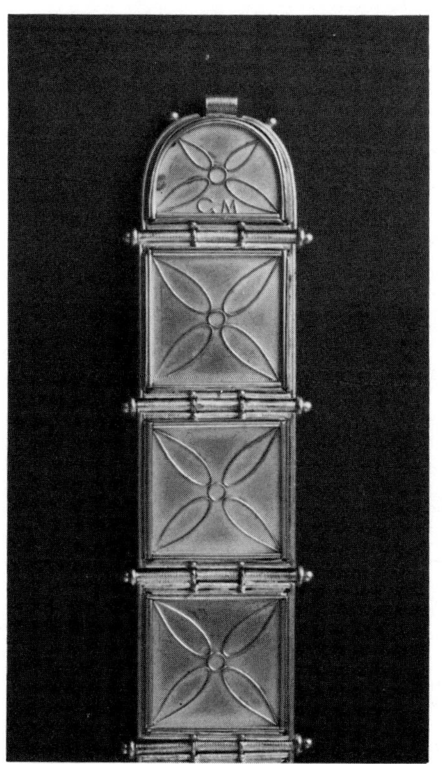

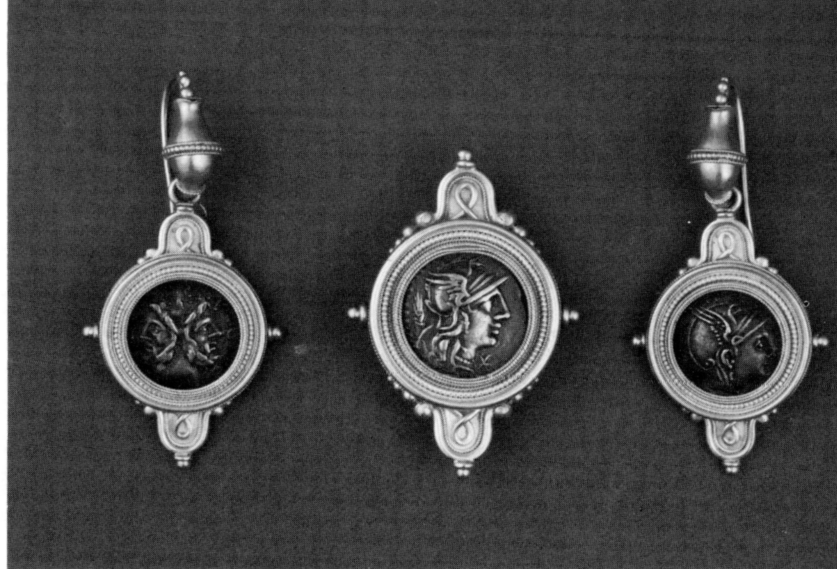

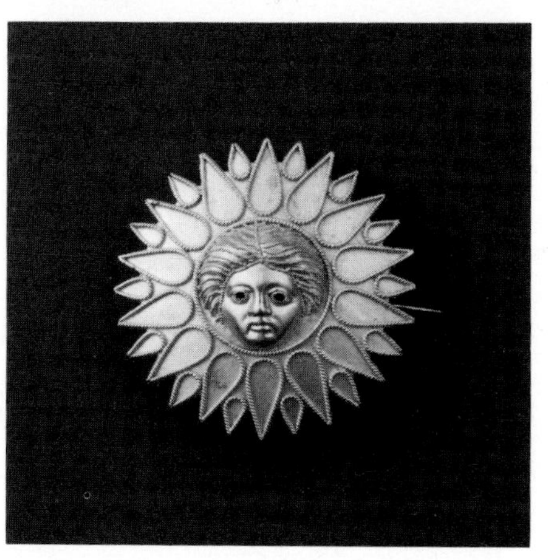

21

Italian 'Archaeological' Jewellery

Bracelet, gold ornamented with granulation and applied wirework. By Giacinto Melillo, Naples, about 1870; reverse, showing the mark, 'G.M.'. L. 19·6 cm.

Demi-parure: brooch and earrings (in the form of rhytons) with coin-set pendants; the brooch set with a Roman Republican silver denarius of the moneyer Cn. Domitius (*c*. 130 BC). Rome, about 1870. L. (brooch) 4·4 cm.

Circular gold 'Helios' brooch, from a Hellenistic prototype dating from about the 3rd century BC, now in the Louvre. By Castellani. Rome, about 1860. D. 3·3 cm.

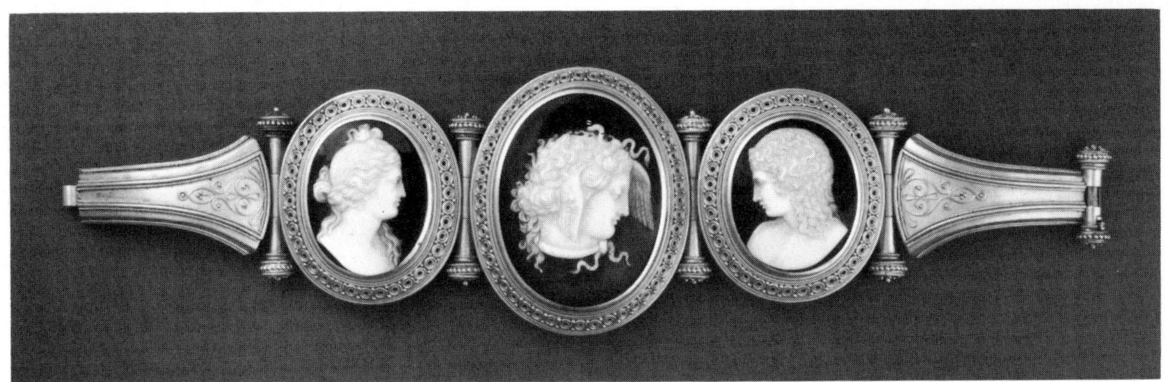

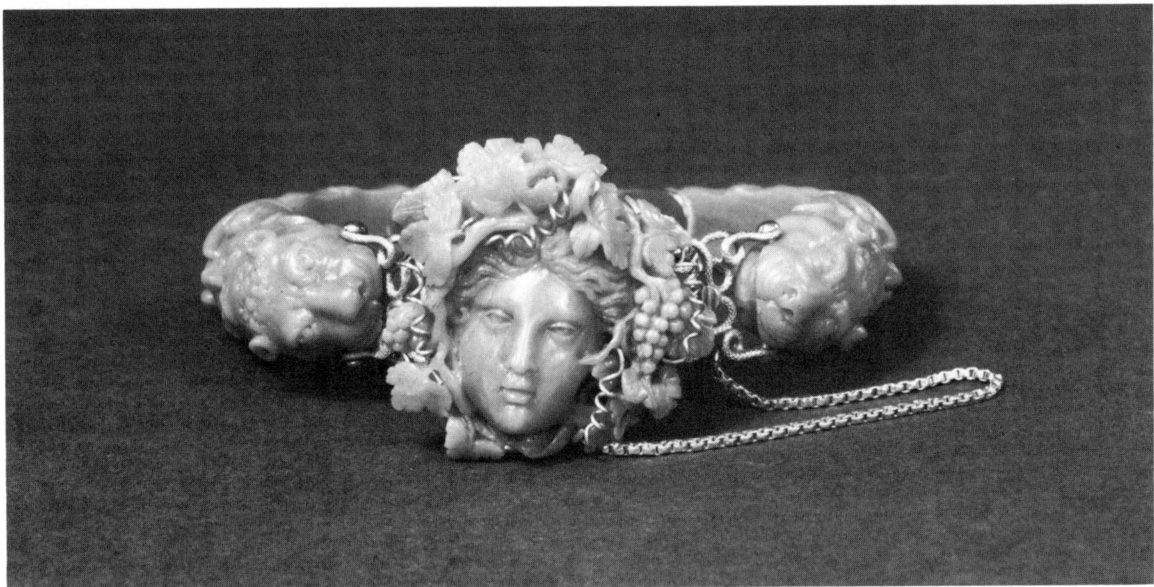

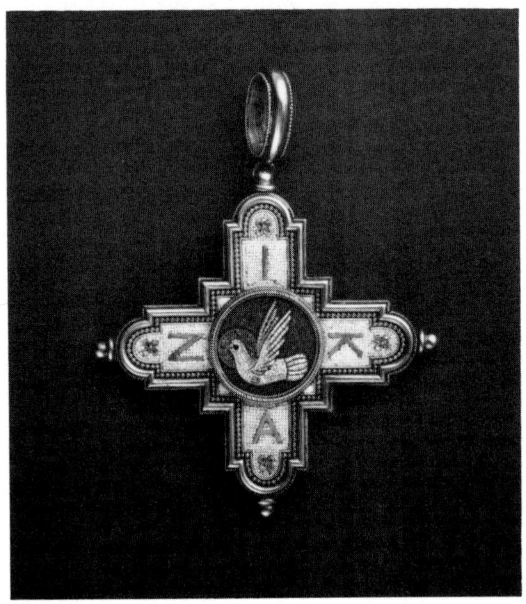

22

Bracelet, gold ornamented with 'Etruscan' style work set with three onyx cameos. By Luigi Saulini. Rome, about 1870. L. 20·8 cm.

Carved coral bracelet, ornamented with gold tendrils. Naples, about 1860. D. 7·2 cm.

Cruciform pendant, gold set with mosaic-work. By Ernesto Pierret. Rome about 1870. L. 6·1 cm.

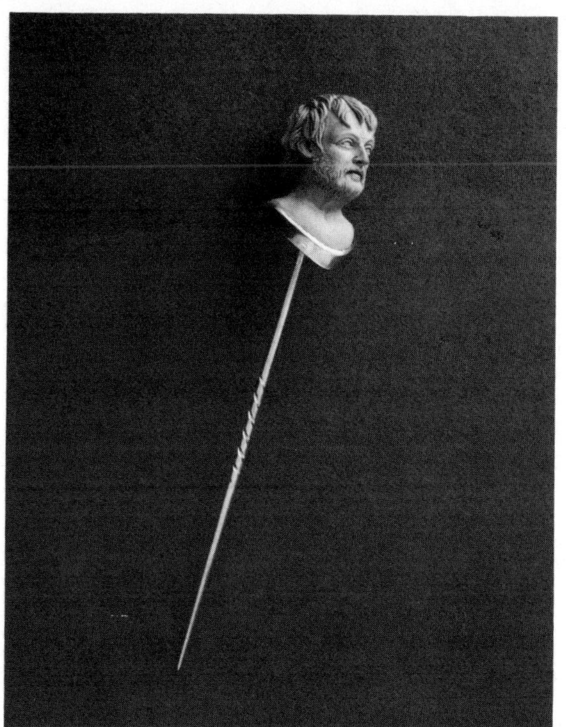

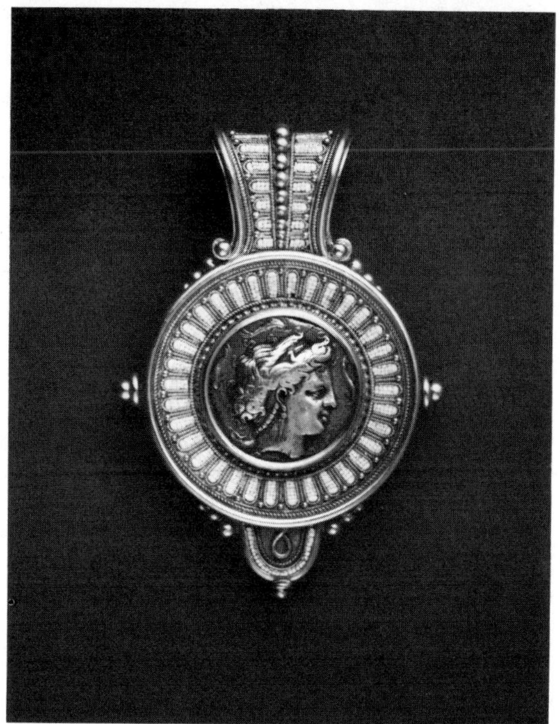

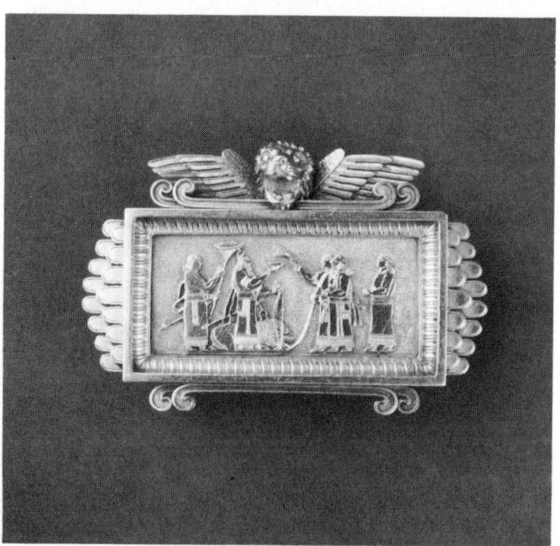

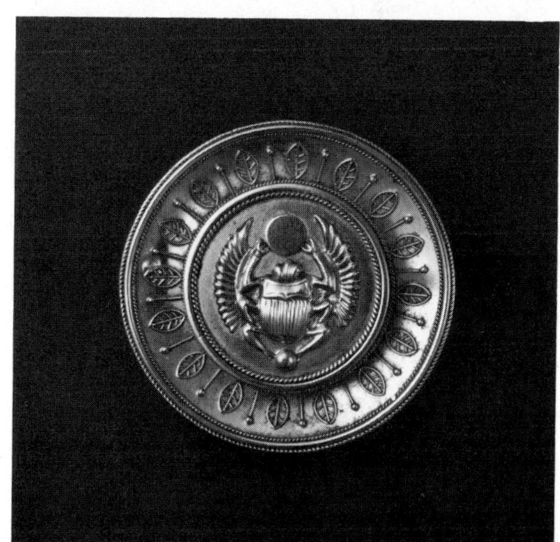

23

Gold stick-pin with male head in carved lava. Naples, about 1850. L. (head) 2 cm.

Pendant, gold with a mosaic-work border, set with a silver didrachm of Neapolis (c. 300 BC). By Ernesto Pierret. Rome, about 1870. L. 6·4 cm.

Brooch in gold ornamented with a copy of an Assyrian relief taken from the throne room of Ashurnasipal at Nimrud. English, about 1850. W. 5·3 cm.

Circular gold brooch in the 'Egyptian' style, in the centre Khepri (the embodiment of Ra, the Sun God). By E. W. Streeter. London, about 1875. D. 4·4 cm.

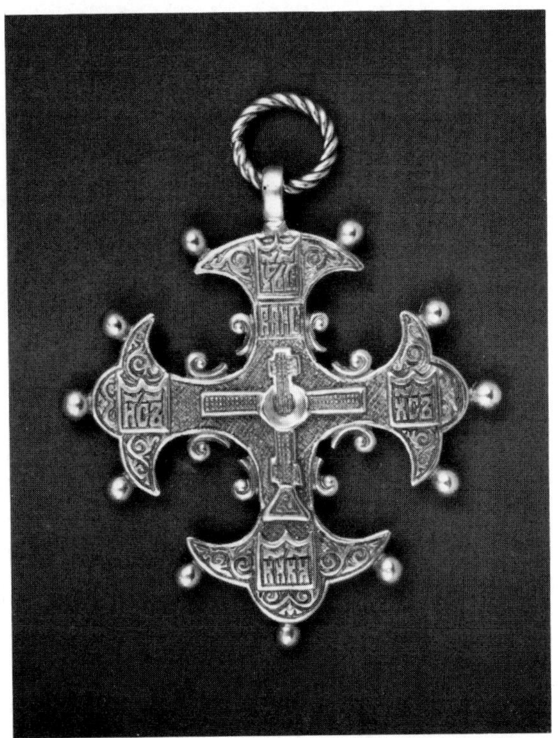

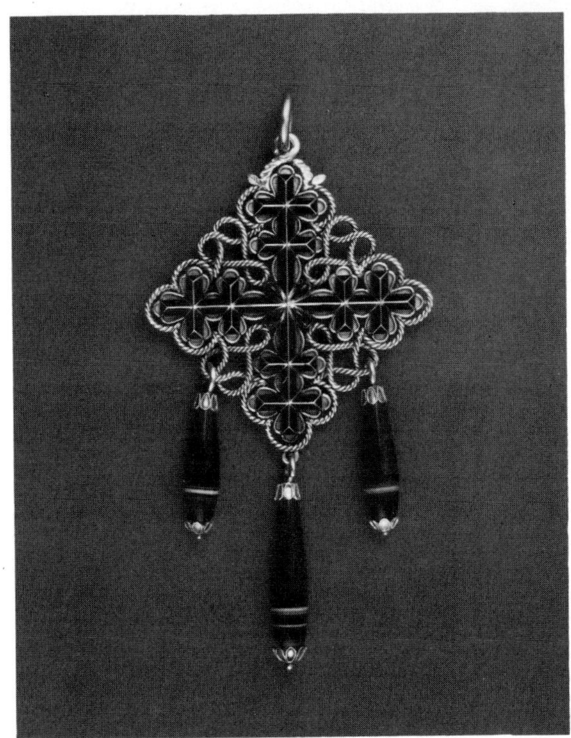

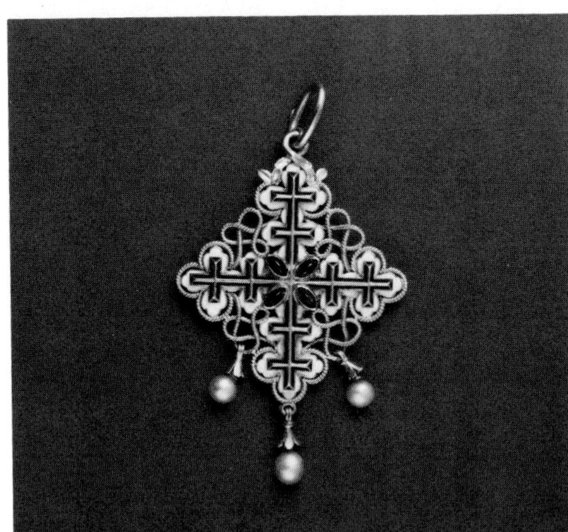

24

Gold cruciform pendant, copy of a Russian pectoral cross of the 16th or 17th century. By John Brogden. London, about 1880. L. 7·5 cm.

Enamelled gold and onyx cruciform pendant, version of pendant below. By Robert Phillips. London, about 1870. L. 10·9 cm.

Enamelled gold cruciform pendant, from a prototype in a portrait of the young Elizabeth Tudor in the Royal Collection. By Carlo Doria, about 1870. L. 7·2 cm.

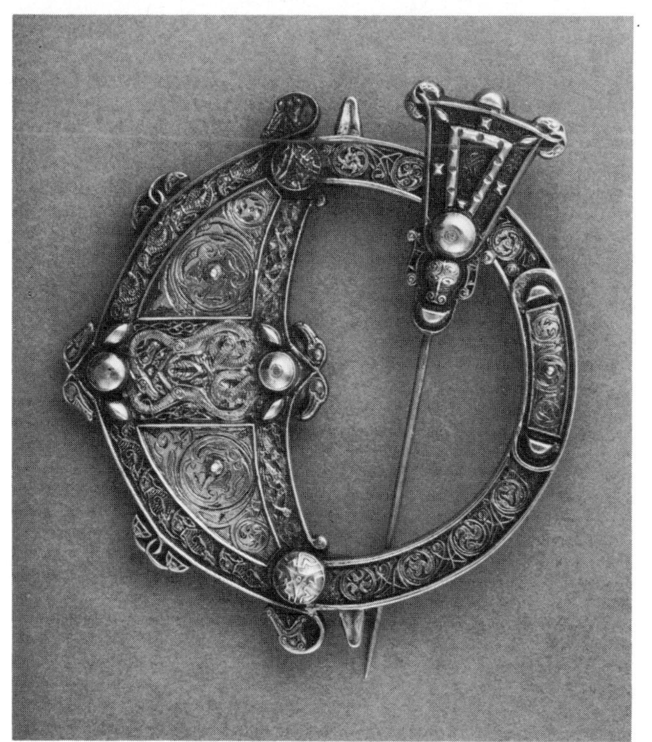

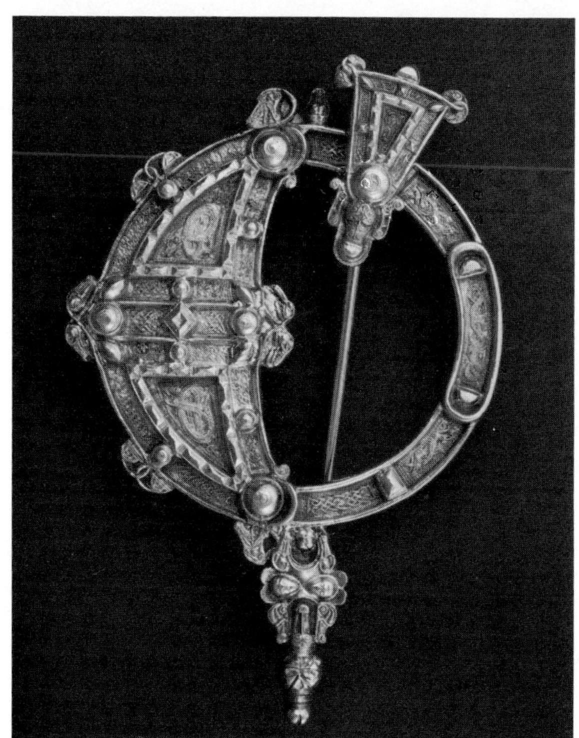

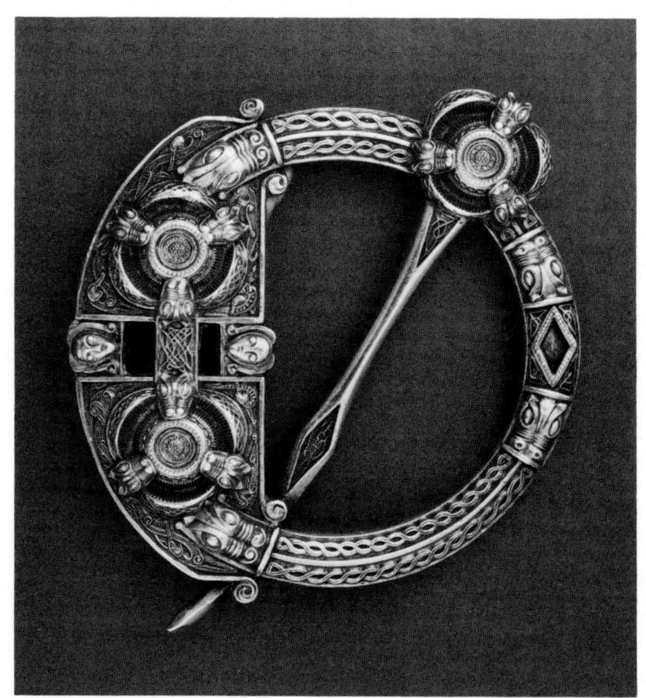

25

Shawl-pin, a version of the 'Tara' brooch, silver. Made by Messrs Waterhouse of Dublin after 1850 (the date at which the firm acquired the original Celtic ring brooch). D. 6·2 cm.

Shawl-pin, silver, parcel-gilt, another version of the 'Tara' brooch, also by Waterhouse. D. 7·1 cm.

Shawl-pin, silver, a version of the Celtic ring brooch found at Co. Cavan. Made by Messrs West of Dublin from the design registered by them in December 1849. D. 5·8 cm.

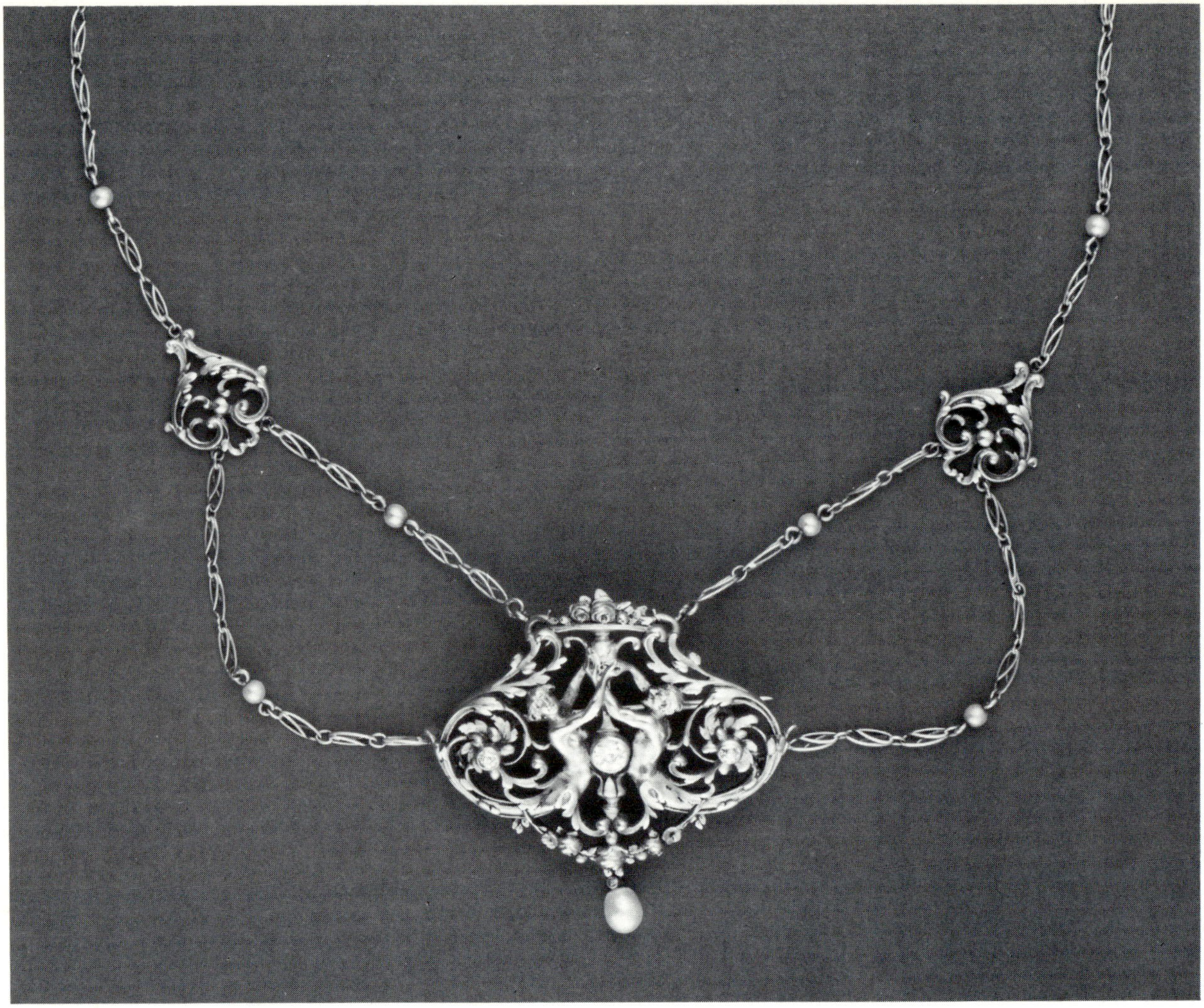

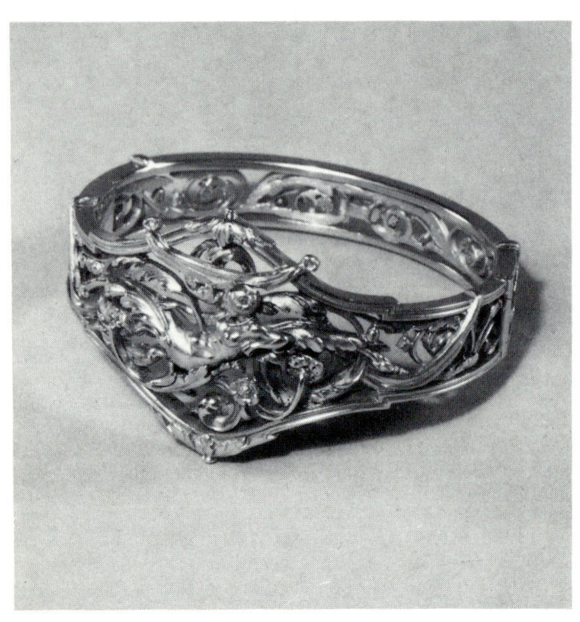

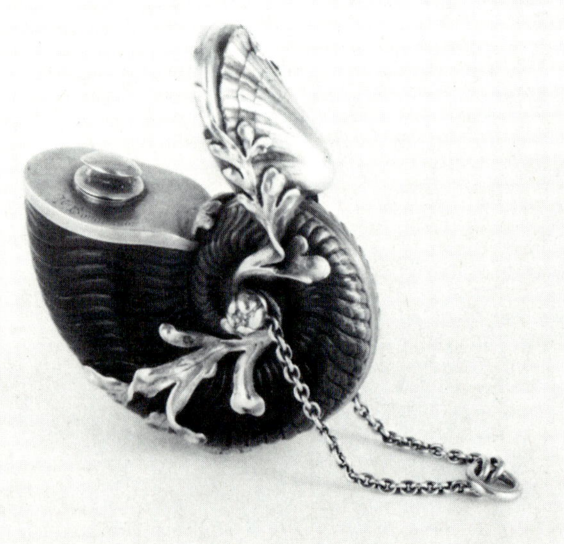

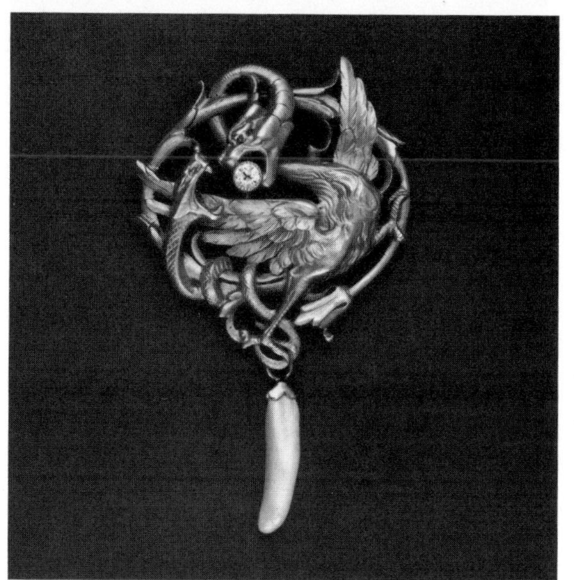

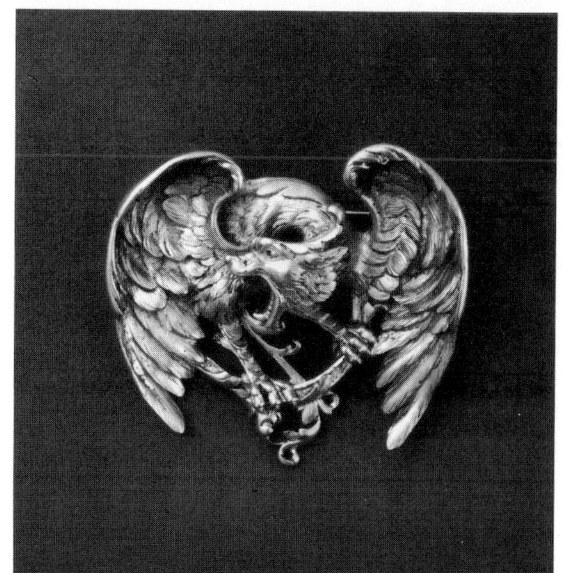

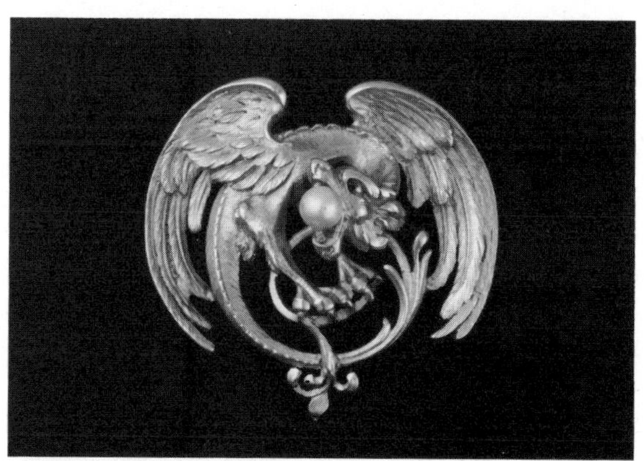

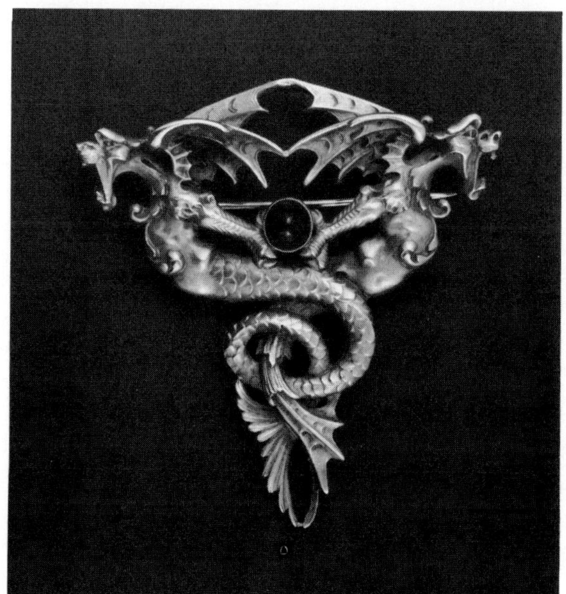

26

Necklace and pendant, gold set with diamonds. Possibly by the Maison Menu. Paris, about 1880. L. (pendant) 4·8 cm.

Bracelet, three-colour gold and silver, in the manner of L. Rault or J. Brateau. Possibly by Boucheron. Paris, about 1880. D. (widest point) 6·6 cm.

Scent-bottle, moulded 'agate' glass in the form of a shell, gold mounts by Boucheron. Paris, about 1890. L. 5·2 cm.

27

Brooch-pendants, cast and chased gold winged grotesque beasts and dragons. French, about 1880. Jules Wièse, Maison Robin and Maison Plisson & Hartz made pieces in this manner. W. 4·8; W. 4; L. 6·2; L. 6 cm.

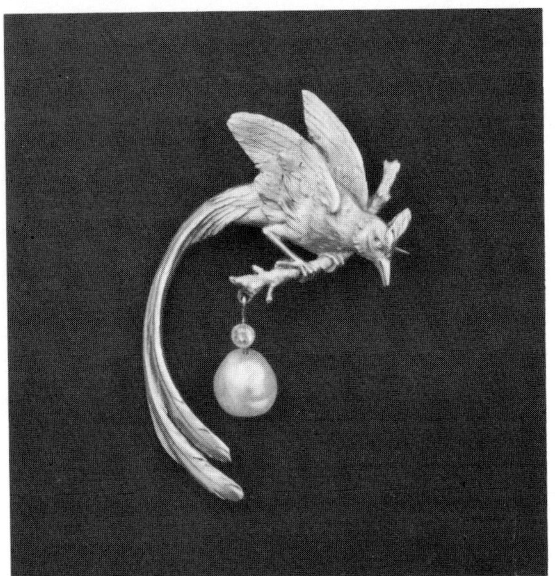

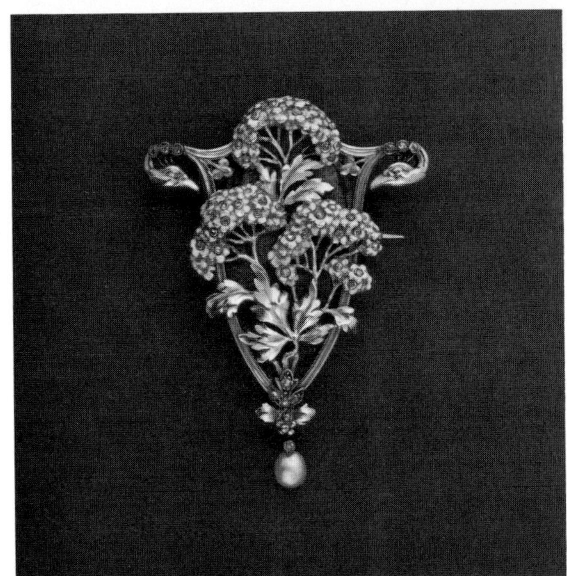

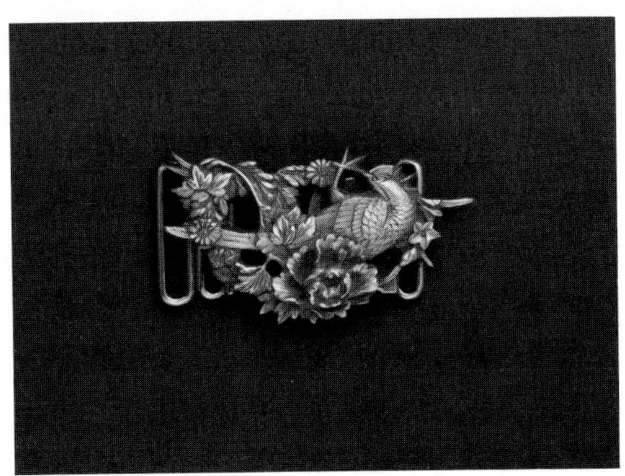

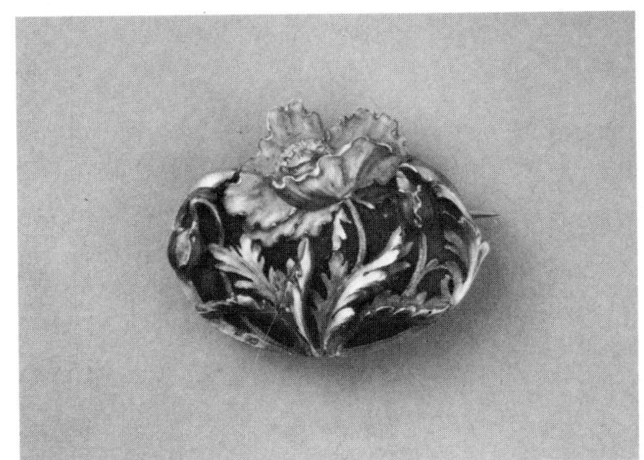

28

Gold bird of Paradise, diamond and peal drop. French, about 1880. L. 5·6 cm.

Enamelled gold brooch-pendant, set with diamonds. By Boucheron, about 1900. L. 5·4 cm.

Bracelet slide, chased gold bird amongst flowers. English (Birmingham) about 1870. W. 3·8 cm.

Gold flower-brooch, *plique-à-jour* and *ombré* enamel. French, about 1900. W. 4 cm.

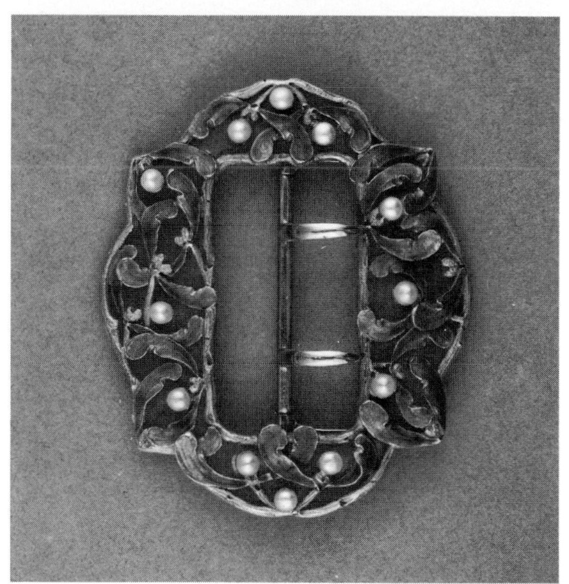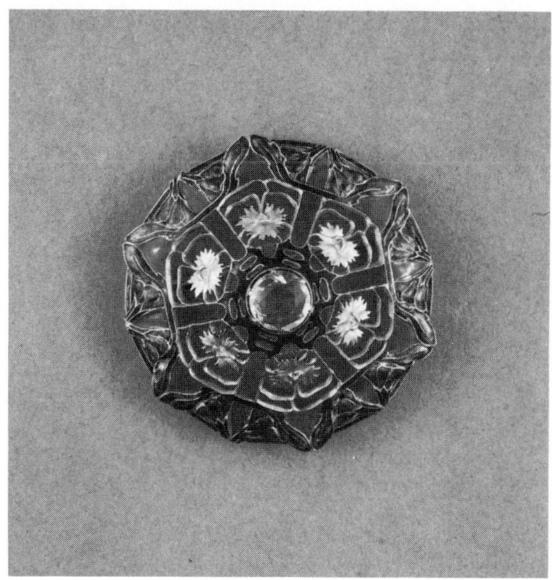

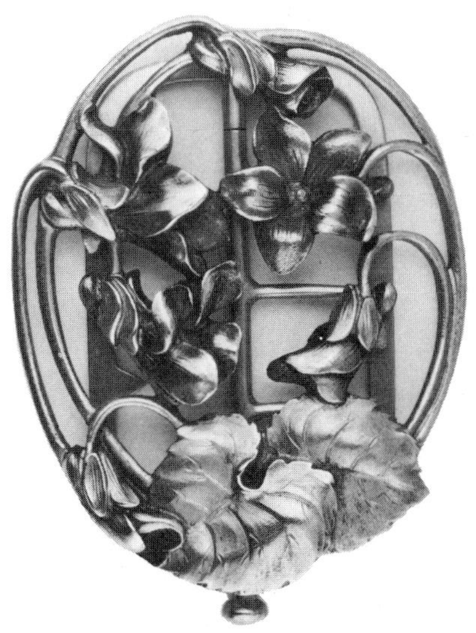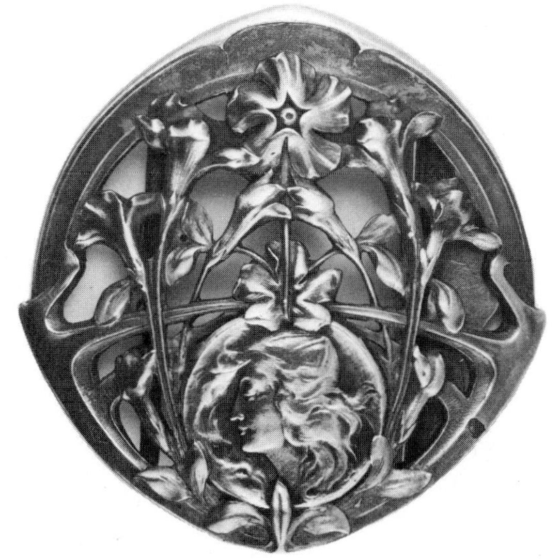

29

Waist-buckle, mistletoe in gold and *plique-à-jour* enamel set with pearls. French, about 1900. L. 5·9 cm.

Brooch, web of flowers and leaves in gold and *plique-à-jour* enamel set with a topaz. By René Lalique. Paris, about 1902. D. 4·3 cm.

Waist-buckle, silver and silver-gilt violets and leaves. Probably by Vever. Paris, about 1900. L. 7 cm.

Waist-buckle, silver and silver-gilt set with a medallion. French, about 1905. L. 7·1 cm.

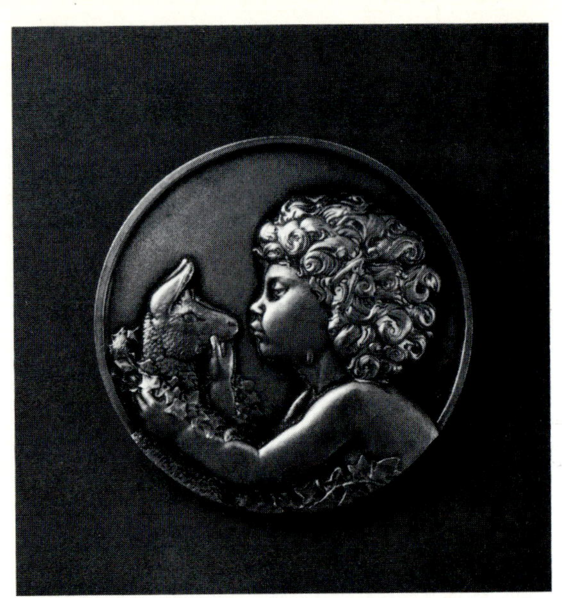
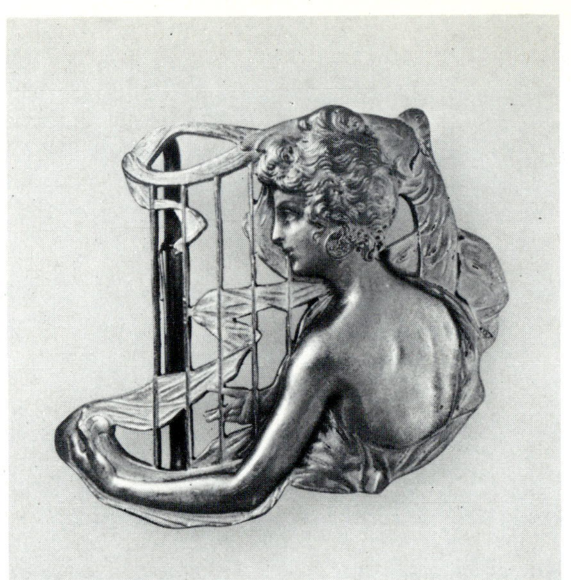
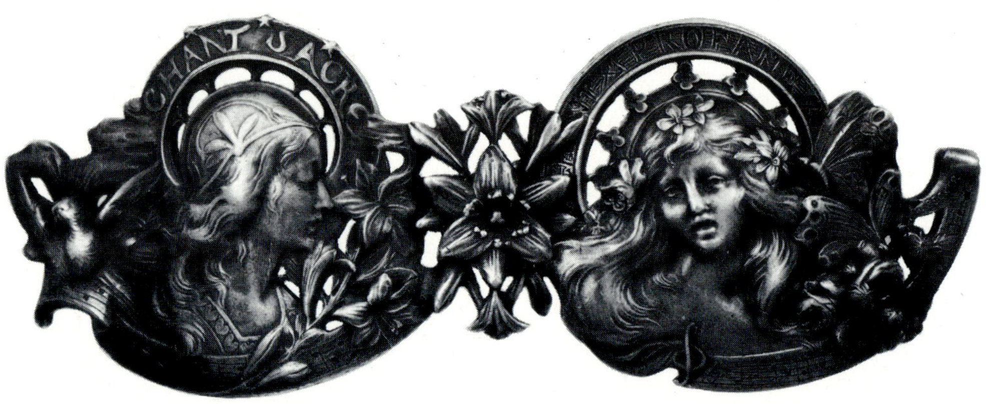
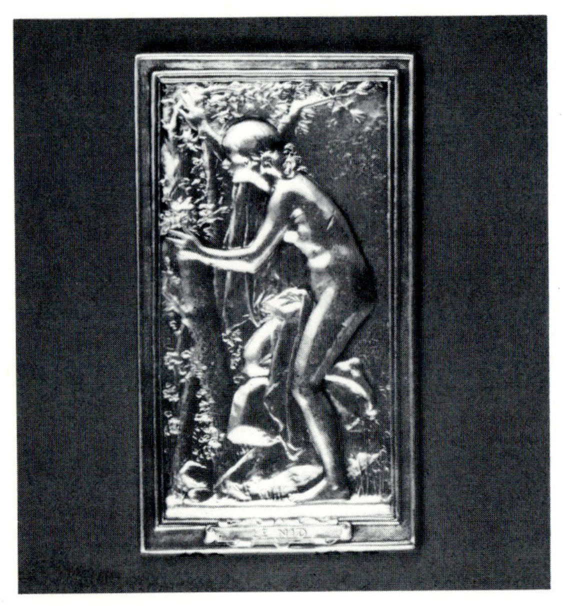
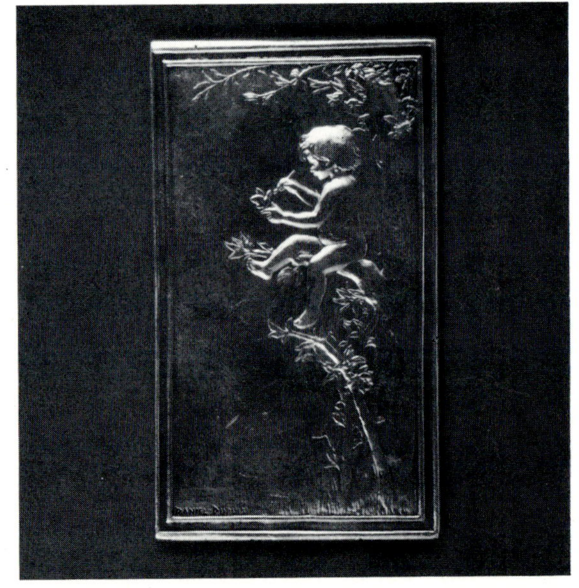

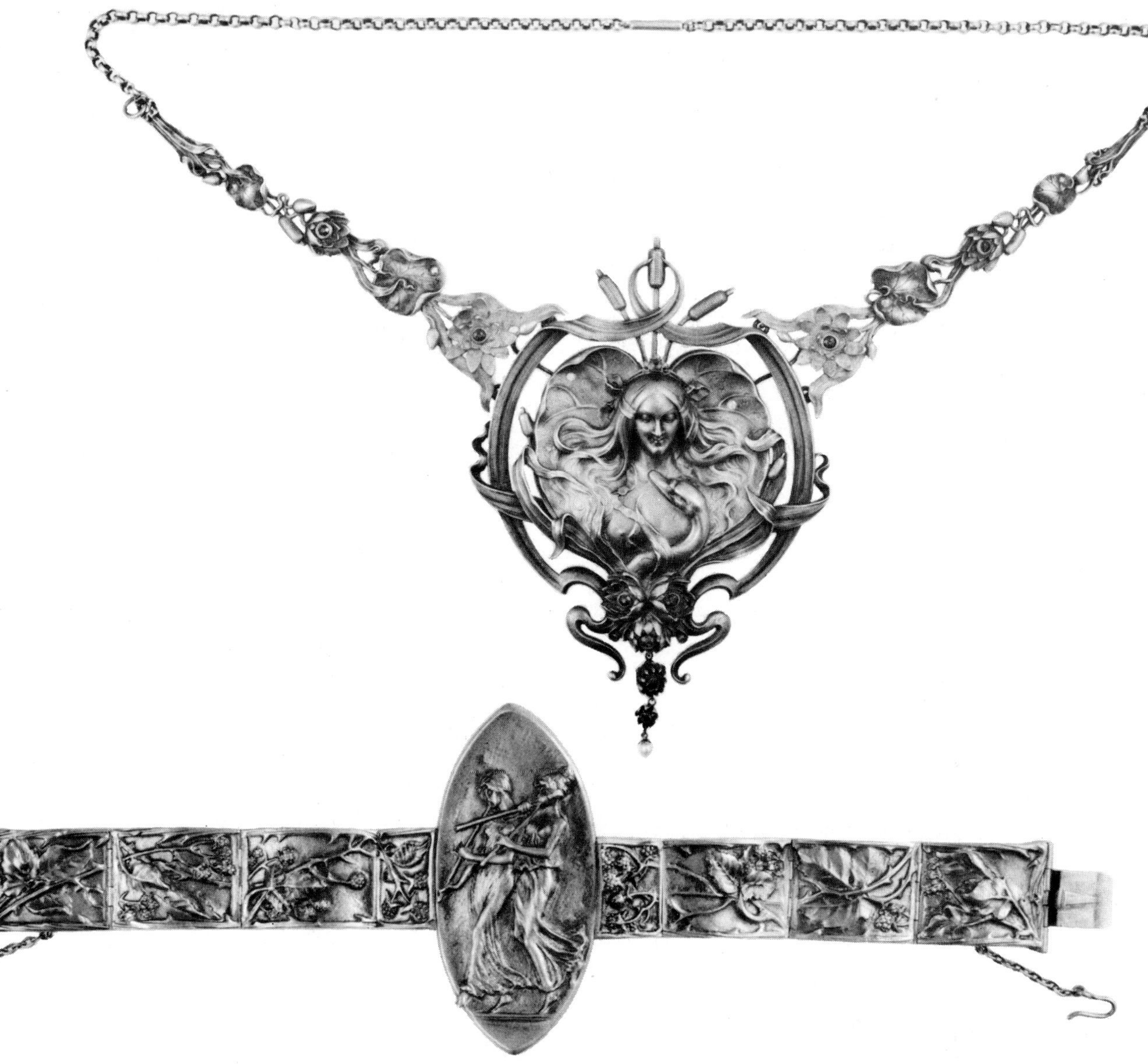

Medallion brooch, 'Pan'. By R. F. Thénot. French, about 1920. D. 5·1 cm.

Waist-clasp, girl with a harp, metal coloured with gold and silver plating. By Piel Frères. French, about 1900. L. 5·3 cm.

Waist-clasp, 'Sacred and Profane Music' (*Chant Sacré*, *Chant Profane*). By Edmond-Henri Becker. French, about 1897. W. 12·1 cm.

'Le Nid' and reverse, from a pair of silver plaquettes entitled 'Le Nid' and 'La Source'. By Daniel Jean-Baptiste Dupuis. French, 1900. Struck for the Paris Centennial Exposition. L. 6·6 cm.

31

Necklace and pendant, 'Leda and the Swan', silver and silver-gilt set with gem-stones, inscribed on the reverse. Swiss, about 1905. L. (pendant) 12·4 cm.

Bracelet, gold, the links chased with branches, the central medallion with dancing figures. By René Lalique, about 1910. L. 18·6 cm.

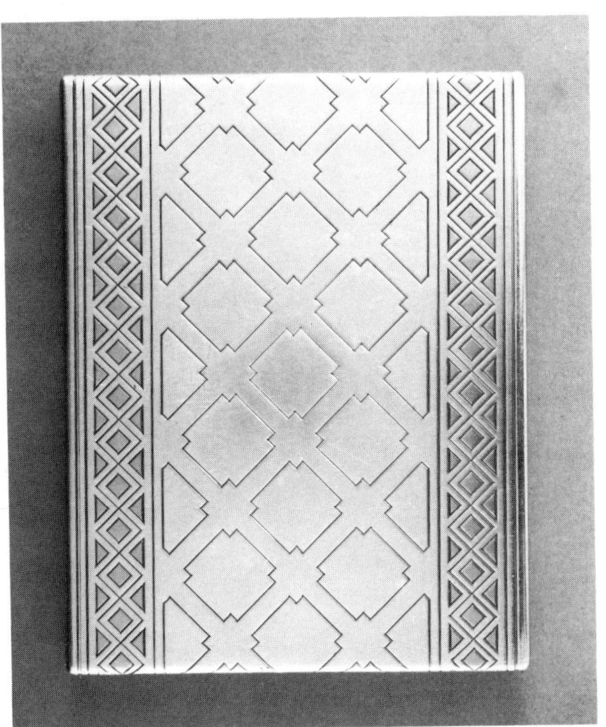

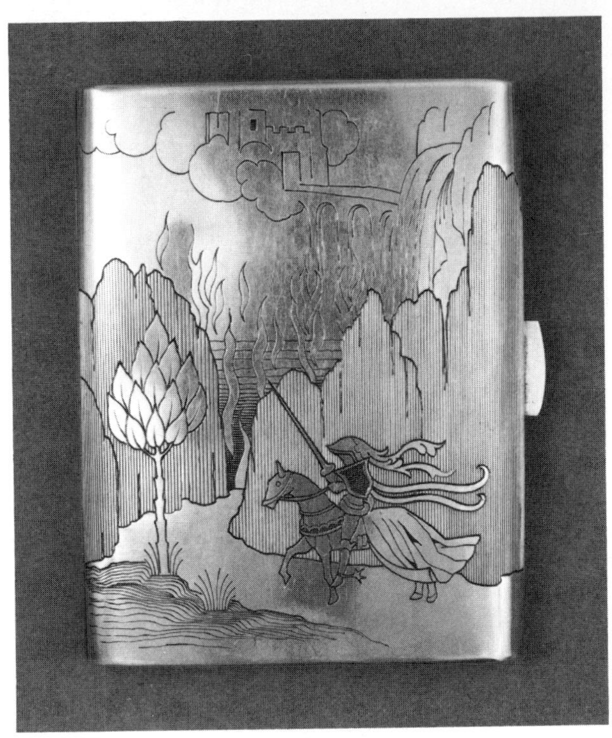

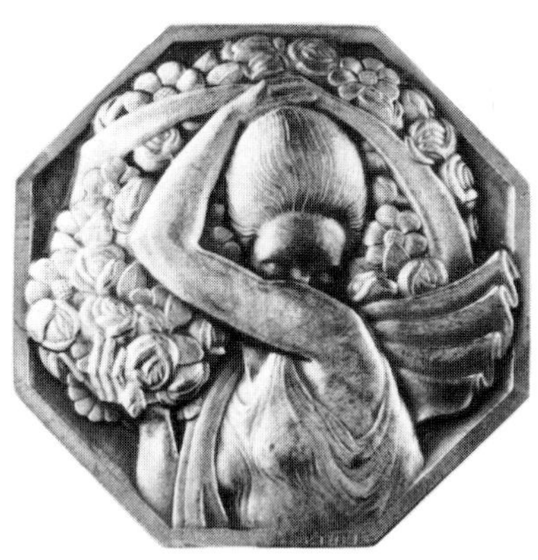

32

Coloured gold cigarette-case by Lacloche Frères. Paris, 1927. L. 10 cm.

Engraved coloured gold cigarette-case by Tiffany & Co., New York, about 1920. L. 7·7 cm.

Octagonal gilt-bronze medallion, signed 'P. Turin'. Paris, about 1925. W. 5 cm.